V

VISIONS AND PRAYING MANTIDS

the angelological
notebooks

Tony Conran

GOMER

First published — 1997

ISBN 1 85902 477 7

© Tony Conran

Tony Conran has asserted his right under the Copyright, Designs and Patent Act, 1988, to be identified as Author of this work.

All rights reserved. No part of this book may be reproduced, stored in a retrieval system, or transmitted in any form or by any means, electronic, electrostatic, magnetic tape, mechanical, photocopying, recording or otherwise, without permission in writing from the publishers.

This book is published with the financial support of the Arts Council of Wales

Printed in Wales at
Gomer Press, Llandysul, Ceredigion

for Peter Hoy

I have always found that Angels have the vanity to speak of themselves as the only wise . . .

The Marriage of Heaven and Hell, William Blake

I'll make you believe in your latter end
I'm an angel above you all.

'The Bitter Withy', folksong

ACKNOWLEDGEMENTS

'The Lyric as an Electrical Field', 'The Muse' and 'The Poem as Symphony' have appeared in *Poetry Wales*. 'Poetry and Musical Form' in an earlier version was published in *Welsh Music*. 'Fairy Tales' and 'The March between Lyric and Tragedy' appeared in *Planet*. 'The Welshness of Things' was adapted from a letter to John Barnie, which accounts for its slightly different tone to the rest. 'The Calling of Poetry,' 'The Lyric as an Electrical Field,' and 'Girl Weeping / Hermes: the Story of a Poem' were distributed by Peter Hoy with the original *Visions and Praying Mantids*.

The painting on the cover 'Icon i Conran' by Victor Neep was suggested to the artist by my reading to him, at his cottage above Rhosgadfan, of my translation of the Elegy for the Last Prince ('Marwnad Llywelyn ap Gruffydd') by Gruffydd ab yr Ynad Coch. Both this painting and 'Interior' on page 65 are in the author's possession and are reproduced with the permission of Phyllis Neep.

CONTENTS

Introduction	11
The Calling of Poetry	15
Factory and Art	18
The Lyric as an Electrical Field	25
Poetry and Musical Form	33
The Muse	43
Girl Weeping/Hermes: The Story of a Poem	58
The World as Asymptote	61
The Painter's Hand	64
Contemplative Poetry	81
The Welshness of Things	98
The Poet's Audience	107
The Poem as Symphony	120
War	134
The Game and the Horror	151
Western and Country	175
Fairy Tales	179
The March between Lyric and Tragedy	187
Angelological. I.m. Peter Hoy, Fellow of Merton	199

INTRODUCTION

Once upon a time, my friend Peter Hoy was a lecturer in French at Leicester University. One of his hobbies was fine printing and small-press publishing. Along with the painter and engraver Rigby Graham his press produced magazines, postcards, small books. He was interested in exploiting a combination of cheap processes like roneo duplication with expensive ones such as letterpress and three-colour printing. He used several of my poems for his publications.

In the early seventies he moved to Oxford as a fellow of Merton, where he found he'd inherited a vast amount of pink, yellow and white duplicating paper. Knowing that I was frustrated by my lack of publishing outlets, he suggested that we should run a sort of journal devoted entirely to my work. It was to be duplicated on unbound sheets, arbitrarily dated and distributed free to people I chose. How he paid the costs I don't know, but who was I to argue?

The idea was quixotic and obviously French in inspiration. French writers seem to comment endlessly on everything in particular and their own work in general; and their journals and intimate notes are gathered and preserved by devoted fans. Our magazine was to include such comments, as well as poems or short essays.

We needed a title. Peter said it should be as fantastic and impenetrable as possible. He asked me to think of one, and I came up with *Visions and Praying Mantids* because of two facts: I had just experienced a waking vision for the first and only time in my life—not a very big one, but interesting and full of comfort; and secondly my zoologist friend Dick Loxton had lent me a praying mantis in a wire cage for a few weeks while he went on holiday. The awful smelly stillness, and then the speed of the beast as she seized her food, were both incredible to me and seemed very relevant to the sort of poetry I wrote.

O.K., said Peter, and then, like all good academics, he suggested it should have a more descriptive-sounding subtitle. It shouldn't be really descriptive, of course . . . Well, I'd always liked the idea of angels—intelligences without such burdensome things as bodies, parents or sex. In fact, I was tempted to think the Almighty had made a mistake when he'd created me not a cherub or a seraph—not even a common or garden angel—but this amphibian creature tied to a body that didn't work and was in any case unreliable in duration. As I pointed out to Peter, an angel is where it thinks. If it thinks of the Statue of Liberty, woof, there it is, balancing on the flaming torch. Quite a good metaphor for our magazine. So it was titled (like this book, except that I now call myself Tony as a concession to democracy):

VISIONS AND PRAYING MANTIDS
The Angelological Notebooks of Anthony Conran

It was published by Peter Hoy at Merton College, Oxford.

Round about a dozen numbers appeared before it became clear that it wasn't working properly. Three things militated against its success. First, I was too garrulous. Faced for the first time in my life with a guaranteed outlet for my ideas, I wrote essay on essay; and it was not (how shall I say?) dainty enough, surreal enough, for what Peter wanted to do. I was being too heavy, in fact. He couldn't keep up, and the issues were coming out later and later.

Second, the lucky recipients of the venture didn't know what to do with the wads of used duplicating paper that kept coming through the post. Instead of treasuring them as holy relics they took the easy way out and trashed them. I have never seen or heard of any of them (apart from my own copies) from that day to this.

The third thing was that Peter ran out of duplicating paper. The whole thing ground to a halt. From time to time I'd take out my collection of pink, yellow and white pages, think 'I must do something with these,' shuffle them round a bit, add the odd essay that seemed to belong; then forget them again.

What emerged when you got rid of the various poems or crusty remarks about the Mona Lisa was the beginning of a systematic deconstruction of bits of my creativity that had served their turn:

mysteries that I wanted to tidy up, programmes of work that didn't last the course, the five-year plans of ten or twelve years back. And from time to time I continued to add to the series. The accretion was slow and uncertain, but gradually a book, a kind of Biographia Literaria, has emerged. It seems impossible to call it anything else but *Visions and Praying Mantids* or to dedicate it to anyone but Peter Hoy.

THE CALLING OF POETRY

To be a highly intelligent, middle-class, spastic child is almost inevitably to be pre-disposed to a feudal view of life. One is in a position of great privilege: every want is supplied, every success applauded. I was hardly cut off by my handicap from taking part in school or play, and learnt to use intelligence and charm to achieve leadership over children younger than myself. I was hardly ever punished—any attempt to do so led immediately to such hysteria and physical breakdown as to frighten any aggressor. In most children the major growing pain is guilt or disillusionment. In me it was shame—the sudden horrifying realization that things were not as I thought they were, and that I had laid myself open to the mockery or pity of people I had intended to impress. The good life was always engineered by others, never by me. If anything went wrong, one screamed in a tantrum and grown-ups put it right. Hysteria—and not melancholia or schizophrenia—became my private escape to unreason.

To say I was spoilt would be true, perhaps, but not in itself enlightening. Spoilt for what? Spoilt as a middle-class child, severely hindered from making a career or a successful marriage. Yes indeed. For along with the privileges of belonging to the professional middle class in a first-world country, there went also in those who brought me up the tacit assumption that I would never have a career and probably never get married. I am sure that if they had been questioned, they would have denied both these assumptions. My grandfather was a Welshman, fanatical about education. I was being educated all right, as if that would enable me to make my own living when I grew up. Everyone hoped I would. But given that I had a great love of learning, a career at the end of it seemed somehow an anticlimax, a pious hope that made no difference to what I was doing. Had my parents—and particularly my father—brought me up in person, this attitude would certainly not have gone unchallenged. But they were away in India, and my grandparents were content to love me, and worry about me, and give me all they had.

I went to grammar school, took examinations, was wangled into university, took my degree. But for me these things never had relevance to any possible career. They were the exact equivalent of being accepted in a noble family as a page, then becoming a squire, and finally being knighted. If one had the particular calling, one did the requisite things. But the calling itself had nothing to do with me. The great need of any feudal individual is to underwrite a sense of vocation with an ideology based on Providence. I became an Anglican in my first year at college, and a Catholic soon after I left.

These things are not extraordinary: many children have a smattering of feudalism about them, many are far more conscious of a vocation than a career. My own vocation was to be a poet. I wanted nothing else, and my desire was answered shortly after my twentieth birthday when I received (so to speak) 'Three Swans on the River of Death,' a poem which told me of the Muse calling me with her fatal power that neither life nor death could dispel. For many years after that, the struggle in my soul was between the Muse and Christ, poetry and God. It would be difficult to imagine a more mediaeval conflict, or one more out of key with contemporary feeling. The goddess was everywhere—in the cry of curlews, in the smile of a girl, in the darkness out of which I created my poems. I did not write poetry because I had something to say. I wrote poetry because it was my calling, what I was born for. A poem was a sign, a talisman, a new-born child. In a sense, I did not even try to make poems, I merely went into the darkness between people where poems were to be found.

Of course, it involved hard work. Sometimes I wrote as many as twenty sonnets a fortnight. Sometimes I waited for months in the gathering despair of not being able to write. The wastage was very large: many poems I rejected the same week, many others reached the wastepaper basket a month or so later. I rarely had as many as twenty-five in my collection at any one time. The occasion of writing was usually given me from outside: someone or something seemed to require a poem. Hardly ever were my better poems written as self-expression or the spontaneous overflow of powerful feelings. I lacked the bourgeois dream of imposing myself on history as a personality or a unique point of view. In the jargon of literary criticism, I never wanted to have my own 'voice'. Of course, I wished to be famous as a published poet, but I thought of my poetry as adding to the deposit—as David Jones would say—much as each new scientist or scholastic philosopher becomes an authority on what is of common concern. What I felt was not usually my conscious starting point when I wrote poems, although, like other adolescents, I churned out my share of emotional confession and sometimes the two activities got confused. On the occasions when I did take my own feelings as my subject, it was not because they were my feelings (or so I thought) but because they illustrated the dealings of God, or Poetry, or Love, with the human soul. It is entirely typical of me as a young man that when I finally fell headlong in love, I should spend the ensuing summer translating Dante's *canzoni* and sonnets: was not Dante the best authority on unrequited love?

Looking back, it is clear that I self-dramatised my feelings in spite of myself. I did not know myself very well in those days. Imagery sometimes betrays me. I expressed myself more, and differently, than I realised. Partly this was a matter of the models that influenced me—Housman and Shakespeare, Rilke, Yeats, Eliot and Graves. But as I got into my stride, I moved more and more towards a feudal kind of poetry, as in the first section of my first book, *Formal Poems* (1960) which were inspired by mediaeval Welsh. I wrote poems to people in order to do them honour in specific situations, like birth or marriage or death. In my time I must have written more serious poems commemorating weddings and birthdays than any other poet in the language.

But even at this stage, the outside world of bourgeois ideology—with its emphasis on decisions, careers, getting married and self-expression—undermined my feudal peace. The shock of hearing my voice on tape, and the painful realization of how peculiar I was, was one such inroad. Another was sexual frustration, a kind of whirlwind that sometimes left me high and dry, exposed to corrosive doubt and despair. And yet a third was the bewilderment I experienced when I was finally ejected from college in 1955 and told to earn my own living. But had I been totally feudal, I think the only recourse would have been to enter a monastery or its modern equivalent, a home for handicapped people.

FACTORY AND ART

I left Bangor at Easter 1955 and started looking for a job, with the help of various government departments pledged to find work for the disabled. For a few months I lived with my parents in Buckinghamshire and then obtained a post at Chelmsford in Essex. I worked for the best part of two years as a clerk. The immensity of it completely bewildered me. Had I continued to work there, it is possible I would have come to terms with it and even learnt the hard way how to work for a socialist future. The only friend I made at the works was a member of the Communist Party; in those days of the Cold War that really meant something. But on the other hand I might have succumbed to the genteel, frightened, attempting-to-be-complacent atmosphere of the white-collar workers I worked with. I had a long way to go before I could accept in myself the insecurity of being a proletarian.

My job—while it bored me—could have been worse. I was called an 'intelligence clerk' which meant I had to read the newspapers, the trade journals and the publications of the Stationery Office, and cut out, circulate and file whatever my boss Mr Sagg told me was of interest to the firm. I was very bad at it, partly because the concept 'being of interest to the firm' had no meaning for me; and partly because it exposed a singular gap in my education. The vast majority of children, it has occurred to me since, learn as a primary skill how to copy what their fellow classmates are doing. Plagiarism is, and ought to be, what education is about. It is a skill that I never acquired. Either I was too bright to need to copy, or I was physically too clumsy to take advantage of anyone as a model. That is, I was either a leader or an idiot, and I had considerable skill as both. But neither of these accomplishments was the least use to an office clerk, where what was needed was simple imitation of what other office clerks were doing.

The crisis came when I was asked to circulate a cutting from *The Financial Times* to various big nobs in the Company. Up to now I had merely suggested articles and pieces of information.

Mr Sagg then agreed or disagreed, and I cut them out and stuck them on pieces of paper ready for filing or circulating round the firm. Now, as a first test of my initiative and keenness, I was asked to circulate something myself. It threw me into panic and consternation. I did not know in the least what was expected of me. Anyone else would have gone to the files where there were literally hundreds of items that had been circulated in precisely this way, and found out what formula to use. I can honestly say that it never occurred to me. Instead, I tried to work it out from first principles, *a priori*. I took all afternoon trying to put the wretched journalese into indirect speech, which was the nearest grammatical skill (and a very difficult one) that I had been taught at school. It obviously wasn't the right way to do it—no business could possibly have survived like that—but I couldn't think of a better. Nobody in the office would help me, and I remember the experience as one of the most unhappy in my life. I don't think my bosses understood how anyone could possibly be so inept, and shortly afterwards I got summoned to Mr Smee's office, a boss a bit higher than my Mr Sagg. He was very gentle with me. He asked me whether there was anything bothering me, whether I was dissatisfied with my position in the firm, and so on and so on. I said no, no, of course not. In fact, the idea that I was dissatisfied (while it was profoundly true) was enormously threatening: I had no idea how I should survive if this job packed up on me.

It seems that my superiors were convinced I was malingering. They were puzzled to find out why. From certain things my mother said, it appears that they contacted her. Mr Smee's secretary used to come and have heart-to-heart talks in my bed-sit. There seems to have been a very noble attempt to rescue me from my friend the Communist. Or perhaps it was their own security they were worried about. He was moved to another factory where I couldn't meet him for lunch and play chess or discuss poetry any more. If only they could have realised how innocent our conversations were, they might have let him eat his dinners in peace.

Now of course all this may be paranoia on my part. I can think of many reasons they might have had for getting rid of my friend—chiefly that he used the time he should have been working on machine-drawings to write poems and flirt with the girls. But I suspect that my friendship did him no good at all; and I regret it very much. A kinder or more colourful antidote to the greyness of Chelmsford would be hard to find. He was a German Jew whose father had been killed in the holocaust; he had escaped to Canada, been locked up as an enemy alien, and then joined the Air Force. He had a Yorkshire wife of great character and a large number of children. He was a serious poet too. One of his poems, 'An Old Hebrew Poet's Musings,' dedicated to me, appeared soon after in *Encounter*. He was originally a Cohen, and he delighted in telling me that he was of the same family as Jesus. At the time I was getting ready to be received into the Catholic Church. He was wonderfully condescending about that!

Partly the company had hired me for the prestige of my degree, but mostly because it had agreed with the government to employ a quota of disabled workers, and I seemed a likely enough lad, given that condition. I rather think they would have liked me to fill one of those safe corners where an old retainer can be trusted to be 'indispensible' without too much jarring of managerial nerves. As I say, I made such a hash of my opportunities that my position as a low-paid clerk seemed absolutely secure, until such time as they could think of an excuse to get rid of me altogether. It was not that I did not try. I tried quite hard, because I have always liked pleasing my superiors and because I dreaded losing my job. I never considered the possibility of getting another one, nor did I know any way in which to evade the do-gooders at employment exchanges in order to take responsibility for my life into my own hands.

* * *

Whimp, or wimp, has become a slang word of the eighties, but as far as I know, when I used it in the middle fifties it was my own invention. I give the poem first in the 1956 version:

THE WHIMP

Poor whimp, his one ambition is
To counterfeit, being inhuman,
Man's plausible normalities;
And therefore drinks, smokes, woos a woman,
And ceaselessly pretends
To know his friends.

He simulates, hopes none will guess
An origin in cuckoospit.
Practised in unexpectedness
And the ripe wisdom of his wit,
One day he may convince—
Or so he thinks.

But we're not fooled. Rooms for a ghost
His love of what we love can buy.
He must despair soon, or at most
Connive to seem man-dead . . . to lie
Unmoulderingly limp—
Alas, poor Whimp!

Here now is my 1989 reworking:

WIMP

His ambition is to counterfeit
the normalities of a man,
the plausible.

He drinks. Smokes. Courts a girl.
The unexpected
ripens his wit.

One day he may convince . . .
Or so he thinks.

But we're not fooled.
Rooms for a ghost
his love of what we love
can buy.

> He must soon despair. At most,
> connive to seem
> man-dead,
>
> to lie
> unmoulderingly limp—
>
> that wimp!

The poem is of course a self-portrait, but I don't think that occurred to me at the time. Had I known I was writing about myself, my conscious mind would have introduced all kinds of unnecessary qualifications, and might indeed have blocked the writing of it entirely. Consciousness seemed to float uneasily along a sea of my suppressed misgivings.

It was during this period that I followed the logic of my upbringing most desperately. I sat in the public library every evening translating Welsh poetry, and I was received into the Church of Rome. These things at least made me feel I belonged. I knew where I was with them, whereas life in the factory and the town where I worked was almost entirely meaningless and bewildering,

Almost, but not quite. For though, when my university college in Bangor offered me a job in its English department, I grabbed it with both hands, some qualms remained. They still do. I wish it had been possible to find my feet as a comrade of those mysterious beings I ate my food with. I suppose, given time, I would have responded to their friendliness. In some capacity or other I could have been acceptable to them. Whether my role would have been reactionary or progressive is beyond conjecture.

What I retain from those months at Chelmsford is a sense of being totally unhinged. Now I can give it names. I can say I was suffering acutely the alienation of the petty bourgeois at being proletarianised. I can recognise the fear of that alienation as one of the most reactionary forces in the world. At the time, though, nobody explained what was happening. I was completely unprepared for the catastrophe and I had no weapons to meet it. Like a village craftsman forced to abandon his independent status and join the workforce in the towns, I clung to my craft and all my spare time was devoted to its pursuit. Translating Welsh poetry was about as useless and atavistic in Chelmsford as shoeing horses or thatching roofs. This is not a comment about translating Welsh poetry in Wales, where it has considerable contemporary relevance; but in Chelmsford—away from Welsh life and even Welsh scholarship—it could have no significance except as a hobby.

Years later, Professor Miles was trying to make a philosophical point and happened to say that some sorts of phrase were too commonplace, presumably, to use in poetry: he gave as an example, 'The grass is green.' I nearly always rise to that sort of challenge. As I sat in the darkness of the immanence of a poem, the memory of clocking in at the factory came back to me as a kind of Dantesque dream—'Give up all hope, ye who enter here.'

FACTORY WORKER

Walks down each his tunnel
past the grey flowers of neighbours'
gardens and last night's party
smelling of must and urine

to where
self must be coagulated
by the pulverising synthetic lights
delivering
with a glanced valediction at the sportspage
husband or father
packaged
to the notating ivory gates,

and behind him
as the day's portcullis drops
and the sun through dirty glass
coughs sarcastically behind him
as the first joke of the day
passes
the first time round—

now behind him
where his children wake and frost the air to school
some centuries behind, the grass is green.

I don't make the mistake of supposing that this is a proletarian poem. It derives partly from the middle-class nightmare of losing caste, partly from middle-class envy of the 'real' experience of the workers; but also, which is why I like it, from a mood, an experience I actually had of clocking into work after a party the night before. I did live through the 'nightmare', I did not merely imagine it. When Bangor offered me a job, I had just accepted the more or less complete alienation of my work; and I had already realised that the sentence was for life.

THE LYRIC AS AN ELECTRICAL FIELD

Like all artistic products, a lyric poem gives our imagination something to live with—almost to live inside, like a house. So of course do novels and plays; but while we can re-read novels and see plays more than once, each time we do so the experience must be more or less complete in itself. We can live with a novel we have only read once—it can be important to us all our lives, even if we read it quite hurriedly in the train between Liverpool and Euston. But a lyric poem practically demands repetition. We can be enchanted, moved or stunned—or just interested or even bored—the first time we read it, but it is like a piece of music in that we don't feel we know it until we do in fact know it almost by heart. This demand on the part of a great lyric is something it shares with slogans, proverbs and parts of the Bible. At its most gnomic, indeed, the lyric approaches these formulaic utterances. But this is not typical: generally a lyric gives us not a formula for behaviour but the key to an imaginative world. It belongs not to the active but to the contemplative life.

A lyric, then, is a structure that demands, and can take, a degree of reiteration that would rapidly reduce most other kinds of discourse to irritating inconsequence. As such, certain things can be said about it. First, it uses words at a high degree of tension. Words vibrate. They spark off each other. The whole structure is an energy-system of high voltage. This of itself would not be enough to make a successful lyric: a political speech could have an equally high verbal potential. And so, second, this energy is structured in such a way as to create space for the imagination or contemplative mind to expand and feel at home. Here are three metaphors: *voltage*, or the capacity of the words to carry meanings and emotions; *lines of force*, or the power of the words to direct our attention; and *electrical field*, or the imaginative space that results in us (as it were) when we activate the structure by reading it or saying it aloud. Clearly, these metaphors are used somewhat loosely. I am not writing a textbook on electricity, and even as metaphors their significances overlap. Nevertheless I find them useful. For example, our first response to a lyric—some kind of undifferentiated shock, either of pleasure or pain—can be seen as the sudden increase of voltage in our verbal awareness, coupled with the fact that the electrical field has not yet reached any sort of equilibrium in our minds.

I

Though voltage is perhaps the most mysterious of these elements, as the nature of language itself is involved, yet it has been subjected to considerable analysis and discussion. Studies of poetic ambiguity, metaphor and various other figures of speech abound. It is what stylistic analysis and practical criticism normally concerns itself with. The entire poetic theory of Ezra Pound is devoted to the concept of poetry as high voltage speech. Perhaps that is why Yeats said that Pound's poetry had style but not form. Voltage is the formal aspect of poetry that is most familiar to students of style, since it provides most of the discriminatory techniques that modulate from one attitude to another as the reader moves through a poem.

II

The lines of force in a lyric are generated by three main factors, closely related: the rhythm or metre, the sentence structures, and the placing of verbs and (to a lesser extent) adverbs, conjunctions and prepositions. The traditional way to write English verse is to talk to yourself—or, quite exceptionally, someone else—in a metrical pattern more or less iambic:

> Five years have past; five summers, with the length
> Of five long winters! and again I hear
> These waters . . .
>   di-dum di-dum di-dum di-dum di-dum

The strength of the English language lies in its verbs and in Shakespeare's day the iambic pattern was able to accommodate most of the verbal structures without undue discomfort:

> I goe, and it is done: the Bell inuites me.
> Heare it not, Duncan, for it is a Knell
> That summons thee to Heaven, or to Hell.

But modern English would not use the simple present, but something like:

> I'll go, and do it. The bell is inviting me.
> Don't hear it, Duncan, for it's a knell
> That's summoning you to heaven or to hell.

Even in such a simple case, the verbs we actually use are working against the iambic; but modern English has developed a system of modal auxiliaries of great subtlety and force:

> I might go. May I go? I must go. Do I have to go?
> I shall have to go. Ought I to go?
> I ought to have been being good ...

It is only by accident that some of these conform to iambic stress. More common are variants of the three-syllable two-stress pattern:

> di-dum-dum

and this pattern is also the product of a totally new kind of vocabulary that is now one of the strengths of the spoken language—again, a rhythm peculiar to the verb. English had two kinds of vocabulary already, derived from Anglo-Saxon and from Latin or French respectively. Now it has concocted a whole new set of synonyms out of verbal particles and adverbs:

> to put off   instead of   to postpone
> to give up   instead of   to surrender
> to put up with instead of   to tolerate

In order to write iambic verse, you have more or less to do without the modern English verb. And since poets are self-conscious about using archaic forms, this in practice means using as few and as weak verbs as possible. It is a useful exercise to go through a few modern English poems, examining the power of the verbs in them. The more iambic the poem, in general, the weaker and more nominal will be the verb-forms. The verb *to be* is a great favourite of the iambicists, since it has not changed its stress pattern much from the eighteenth century. There is also a horrid tendency to overuse the radio commentator's simple present:

> Lady Diana moves down the aisle and takes her position beside the Prince of Wales . . .

This is supposed to make the poetry more vivid, but usually dusts it with the tarnish of the academic exercise. Its metrical *raison d'être* is all too obvious: the simple present is one of the few verbal forms that are still easy to use in iambics.

One can quite easily concoct a metre based on the di-dum-dum foot:

> I might get a Rolls Royce and give up my yacht
> And sell out on Wall Street at five grand the lot -
> di-dum-dum di-dum-dum di-dum-dum di-dum

The trouble is, the stressing is metrically unstable. What normally develops out of such a rhythm is the lumbering Victorian amphibrach or anapaest, with a stress on every third syllable; and this nineteenth century solution to the problem of the non-iambic verb is unsatisfactory on four grounds. One, it does no justice to the delicate equilibria between the double stresses in the verb forms found in speech. If one says 'I might get a Rolls Royce' naturally, there are many possible inflections one can use; but in the amphibrachic line concocted above, only the clumsiest stressing is indicated. Two, the three-syllable foot allows the vigour of the verb, checked by the iambic, free play, but at the cost of imposing an anapaestic prolixity on the other parts of speech, which in general still seem to crystallize best in two-syllable feet rather than three. Three, the rhythm itself seems somehow too facile to be an adequate medium for poetry. And four, it is much too much a mere adaptation of iambic habits of feeling to break the new ground that is required.

There is no reason at all why stress should have to be the main organising feature of English poetry. Any feature of the spoken language whatsoever can be used to organise a poetic structure, given an adequate system of notation. A line can be based on the number of stresses, the number of syllables or the number of words; it can rely on the alternation of phrases, or on the accumulative effect of similar sentence structures. One can build up blocks of lines related to one another in many different ways, the lines in each block having different relations among themselves, perhaps, but the overall effect having some kind of symmetry. Or the verb forms themselves can be used like keys in music, to build up complex symphonic patterns such as sonata-form or rondo, with modulation from one modal auxiliary to another having as clear-cut a formal role as the change from one tonic to another in the symphonies of Mozart. Again, punctuation is a way of notating intonation patterns and pauses; and I have sometimes tried the experiment of starting to write a poem by choosing the punctuation marks I would allow myself, and writing the words around these. For example, two pairs of brackets would enclose two stanzas of three lines each, each being preceded by a stanza of five lines unbracketed; the whole structure of sixteen lines being a single complex sentence.

This kind of analysis lies behind many of my *Poems 1951-67*. I have been trying to explore the formal possibilities of the language as a medium for poetry. I suppose this effort is not much to present taste; but actually it is a fascinating business, continually opening up new expressive possibilities. Nobody doubts that English verse is in a mess, yet nobody does anything about it, except trust their own ears. As the iambic base more and more crumbles, this means in fact that the English ear is losing its sensitivity to verse as such. Trusting to the judgement of the ear, therefore, in the absence of rational analysis, is likely to make the problem worse, not better. Had English been a purely parochial speech, like Lithuanian or Welsh, I have no doubt that its metrical structures would have kept pace with its linguistic development. (It is interesting in this connection that the verb in Lallans does not seem to have got out of hand as it has in standard English, so that vigorous iambic verse is still the natural medium for poets in Scots.) But English is the speech of half the world, and it is used to communicate so much that is fake or insincere, or humanly neutral at least, that it has almost lost its bearings as a living language. Wyatt after the civil strife of the fifteenth century Wars of the Roses confronted just such a metrical no-man's-land. His chosen weapon was the Italian sonnet and the ten-syllable line. I work on a broader formal front, but then my situation is more desperate.

III

A lyric's electrical field is what gives gives it the feeling of having three dimensions, so that you can, as it were, walk round it like a sculpture. It stands in its own ground. One way a writer can achieve this is to present two or more different time-sequences in close juxtaposition to one another, much as one way of presenting three-dimensional space in a painting is to build up vertical planes one behind another, parallel to the picture-surface. The poet can use the tenses of the verb as the artist uses perspective—for example the juxtaposition of past and present in Goldsmith's 'The Deserted Village' or the use of different pasts, and finally the present, in Wordsworth's 'The Two April Mornings.' Another, and better way, because it is using the solider aspects of language itself, is to develop the force of some of the nouns, until they seem to occupy their own three-dimensional space which the poet can then connect up with his lines of force to present a total three-dimensional pattern. The figure of speech known as personification often has this sort of function. But by far the best device that the lyric poet can use to make his work stand up in three-dimensional space is to exploit the threeness that is inherent in the language itself: I mean of course that of the three grammatical persons—I—you—he, she or it. If I had to choose any single aspect of the art that a young poet ought to master, it would certainly be the most economical handling of the three grammatical persons, and particularly the second since that is the one which most of all creates a sense of confrontation and therefore depth.

And it is precisely in this skill, and therefore in the spiritual dimensions that this skill implies, that so much modern poetry, whether romantic-suburban or symbolist schizoid, fails so dismally to create a three-personed space, except now and again in purely intimate contexts. A marxist critic would see this as the nemesis of the cash-nexus in action: all other human relationships are gradually submerged into the mysterious neuter of the market, so that they become 'objective' and quantified in terms of money. The absurd Cartesian position that the individual is somehow prior to the society of which he is a part means that society becomes a puzzle, explicable only in terms of some form of social contract that the individuals make between themselves. The outward and visible sign of this contract in capitalist society is obviously cash; and therefore cash, not personal confrontation, becomes the public reality, softened to more sensitive souls by the personal oasis of private life. To some extent, of course, romanticism began as a rejection of this position. Wordsworth's *Lyrical Ballads* are full of genuine I-thou relationships. Other individuals were still felt as allies or enemies: the romantics still used , indeed over-used, the vocative case—'O friend,' and so on. But as real power passed from individuals (as individuals, that is, for they could still wield power as officers of a corporation or state), so did the romantic imagination cease to involve its possessor in relationships other than intimate and private. In the suburbs nowadays, the only you's are the intimates who form a bulwark against the defects of loneliness.

Still less does the poetry that arises out of monopoly capitalism in the age of the limited liability company involve real I-thou relationships. In the romantic-suburban poets you do at any rate find poems to a wife, or a child, or a parent; but in the symbolist-schizoid (with rare and lovely exceptions like Allen Ginsberg's 'Kaddish' for his mother Naomi) all you get is the invocation of the *'hypocrite lecteur!—mon semblable,—mon frère!'* The reader is invoked as a conspirator, a shadowy fellow-consumer; it is assumed that his identity is as unreal and as schizoid as the poet's, of whom indeed he is a mere projection. The accents of men talking to men are far away—

> No place of grace for those who avoid the face
> No time to rejoice for those who walk among noise and
> deny the voice.

Such confrontations as there are in this poetry remind one of the interviews in television adverts. Humanly, their meaning is nil, deliberately staged to mystify or reinforce the fatuousness of salesmanlike techniques—'There's something going on here, and you don't know what it is—do you, Mr Jones?'

Since the lyric poem of the past, in the overwhelming majority of cases, was specifically an art of I and thou, this contemporary deprivation is comparable to the loss of melody from modern art-music or the loss of the human figure from modern sculpture and painting. I should judge all three deprivations to arise from a single cause, a basic reluctance to take anyone seriously except oneself and those who are essentially mere projections of oneself.

POETRY AND MUSICAL FORM

I cannot remember a time when music, of some sort or other, was not important to me. As a child I used to lie in bed listening to my cousin singing the songs he had learnt in school, urging him to sing more and more until the exasperated grown-ups put a stop to it with dire warnings. I fell in love with Schubert's *Unfinished*—it was the first love of my life and love at first sight at that—at the age of fourteen. Every detail of that love affair is still vivid in my mind. When I hear the *Unfinished* now, it has the smell of my aunt's sitting room in Liverpool where I first heard it—the blue Columbia labels of Beecham on three 78s that I made my aunt play fifteen times a day, till she refused to put it on again no matter what I said. Music has this inordinate lust for me, even now. Or at least, some music has. Sometimes I can retire into Irish piping or Indian ragas for a whole day at a time, and emerge happy and shattered, to plague my friends with incoherent descriptions and invitations to share in the wonder.

It is difficult to know where to start. As I write a friend from Derry has arrived out of the blue and is practising a ballad upstairs. So that seems a fair enough place to begin. The sung word, to a tune repeated over and over, the static circling of an idea round a simple melodic repetition—this is the place I start at, as European lyric itself did, with the dreamlike concentration of the troubadour *canso*. Finally, despite every incitement to move and struggle and dramatise, it is that feeling of a 'still point in a turning world' that still totally grips me. In my heart of hearts, the adoption of equal temperament, which made dynamism and drama and sonata form possible in music, I think of as some kind of necessary disaster, like original sin, which I would fain repent and disregard. Perhaps that is why I've always been drawn to folk music, as well as the unaccompanied chants of plainsong and the monodies of the troubadours.

One of my delights as a poet is to hear my own words sung, but unfortunately I find writing songs very difficult. Perhaps my own complete lack of a singing voice is too much of a hindrance.

Only one song I've written has been sung in Bangor for more than a week or so. It is called 'The Ghost' and a student called Joy found a tune for it—a great slow air—which made it almost viable as a folksong in student folk clubs:

> The cumbrous coat of mist I carry
>   Each leg is of the rough-hewn stone,
> Arms a-swing like a weathercock turning,
>   Tongue of me frozen to the palate bone.
>
> 'Shall I not kiss you this fine midnight,
>   As your smiling lips invite at last?'
> Arms a-swing like a gibbet turning,
>   Heart of me frozen to time that's past.
>
> 'Shall my hands not reach to your body,
>   So warm the little breasts and sweet?'
> A crown of brambles to dry dust crumbles,
>   Wound of a nail through my hands and feet.
>
> 'Shall my love be to you welcome,
>   As never it was in time before?'
> The cumbrous coat of mist I carry
>   Stands fathom-tall within your door.

The basic problem, I suppose, is that the complex imagery leaves you in doubt (and not just in performance) who the ghost is—the poet himself or Christ? And if it is Christ, as the third stanza implies, what are the implications of his haunting the girl? Who is she? Mary Magdalen? The Soul? Nothing quite fits. Or is it simply the poet identifying with Christ? As a *revenant* ballad, it is topheavy with unanswered questions.

It illustrates, though, the characteristic tensions of my apprentice poetry—say, up to 1958, when I was twenty-seven. Most of it was strophic, based on iambic rhythms: that is to say, metrically it represented a static turning of a single tune, whether simple, like this song, or complex, modelled on the Italian *canzone*. I did not always use rhyme, and sometimes I employed syllabic rather than accentual metres; sometimes I wrote free verse. At other times I used binary forms like the sonnet (A B, as musical critics put it) or a series of different but related measures (A B C D . . .). These contrasts tended to be like that of a Prelude and Fugue, one after the other, not built into the fabric of the whole like the opposition between first and second subjects of a sonata. The contrast was extrinsic, not intrinsic. It had no dialectic force, and therefore could only support variation and not true development in the symphonic sense.

At the same time, the imagery works against this static turning on a single axis—in 'The Ghost,' for example, you don't know who the ghost is, which makes it hard to rest easy in the pattern. It was this unclarified quality of many of my early poems that made readers complain it was 'too intellectual' for them. As usual with such complaints, the problem was exactly the reverse of what they said. My poetry was not yet intellectual enough. Intelligence makes things clear, not obscure.

In 1959 I started to experiment with the musical forms that developed out of equal temperament—i.e., sonata form above all, but also sonata-rondo and more developed, freer kinds of music, based on wandering modulations from one key to another. Could they have any equivalent in poetry? Not in the traditional metres, certainly; or at least, not if these were the only formal principles at work. But of course they are not. Not even in the most rigid and difficult stanza-form does the poet rely only on metre and rhyme to organise his material. There are always other parameters: the logical structure, the syntax, and the kind of language being used. For example, Marvell's poem 'To his Coy Mistress' is organised metrically in rhyming couplets of octosyllabic lines. But this counts very little more than a time signature. What organises the poem into three more or less equal movements is the logical structure:

> A. Had we but world enough and time
> This coyness, lady, were no crime . . .
>
> B. But at my back I always hear
> Time's winged chariot hurrying near . . .
>
> C. Now therefore . . .
> Let us sport us while we may.

This in turn gives rise to a syntactical sequence: the first section is in the subjunctive mood (of impossible condition), the second is in the indicative, and the third is in the imperative. If the metrical structure corresponds, in this case, more or less to a time-signature, then the control exercised by the moods of the verb is much more like that exercised in music by key and mode. Just as a minor key is likely to produce a different kind of musical experience from a major, so the subjunctive gives rise to a different poetry from the indicative.

The poem shows Marvell *consciously* exploiting logic and syntax to shape a structure larger than a metrical unit. But sometimes the shaping seems largely unconscious. A typical example of quasi-musical form operating at a subconscious level is Wordsworth's 'Highland Reaper', which in effect is in sonata form, despite the fact that Wordsworth might never have heard a classical sonata, let alone analysed its structure.

Sonata or first-movement form is a piece of music divided into three sections—or more if you observe all the repeats. First, the exposition usually presents two contrasting 'subjects' or clusters of 'motifs' in two contrasting keys. Second, the development explores the musical basis of the two subjects and the tensions between them, often in very adventurous harmony. And third, the recapitulation more or less repeats the exposition, but this time in the same key throughout: the second subject is reconciled to the first. A fourth section, the coda, usually concludes the piece with a resounding reassertion of its opening key. This account of the form is very rough, and you could probably find exceptions to anything in it. Sonata-form was practically obligatory in the first movement of a classical sonata or symphony.

In 'The Highland Reaper,' the first stanza corresponds to the 'exposition': it is in the imperative for the first subject, whose three motifs are 'solitary,' 'reaping' and 'singing'; and in the present indicative for the second, with two motifs, 'melancholy' and 'overflowing':

> Behold her, single in the field,
> Yon solitary Highland Lass!
> Reaping and singing by herself;

> Stop here, or gently pass!
> Alone she cuts, and binds the grain,
> And sings a melancholy strain;
> O listen! for the Vale profound
> Is overflowing with the sound.

One could particularise further: line 5, for example, is a bridge passage modulating from the imperative to the indicative but using material already stated—for 'alone' is equal to 'solitary' and 'cuts' and 'binds the grain' an expansion of 'reaping.' The way the indicative in the seventh line is momentarily interrupted by the return of the imperative ('O listen!') is very Beethoven-like, to my ears.

Partly the tension is between an imperative which is directed at some hypothetical 'you,' and an indicative, which postulates statements about a 'she.' The opposition cuts very deep into the formal structure of the language.

The next two stanzas form a long development section, using the five motifs in various unlikely contexts: nightingales in Arabia, cuckoos breaking the silence of the seas in the Hebrides, old unhappy far-off things, familiar matter of today, etc. As in any good symphony, this forms the imaginative core of the work. First we have a development of the first subject, or at least two of its motifs, the 'solitude' and the 'singing,' but the tense is the past indicative, in the negative. The poet is using a figure of speech akin to hyperbole, describing his subject by denying that anything quite like it ever happened before:

> No Nightingale did ever chaunt
> So sweetly to reposing bands
> Of Travellers in some shady haunt
> Among Arabian sands:
> No sweeter voice was ever heard
> In spring-time from the Cuckoo-bird,
> Breaking the silence of the seas
> Among the farthest Hebrides.

The 'singing' motif is then combined with those from the second subject—particularly the 'melancholy' of course, but notice how the word 'flow' brings in the 'overflowing' of line 8. The tense is now present indicative, but with more than a hint of the subjunctive. Notice how the interrogative construction ('Will no one tell me?') implies the hypothetical 'you' of the opening imperative:

> Will no one tell me what she sings?
> Perhaps the plaintive numbers flow
> For old, unhappy, far-off things,
> And battles long ago:
> Or is it some more humble lay,
> Familiar matter of today?
> Some natural sorrow, loss, or pain,
> That has been, and may be again!

The 'reaping' motif is only present as a kind of background, perhaps part of the 'familiar matter of today'; but the 'melancholy' and, again, the 'solitude' (for there is no one to tell him what she sings) are given the full imaginative treatment.

Had this been music, the recapitulation would have returned to the first key of the piece. That is, the fourth stanza would have been in the imperative mood. But tenses and moods of the verb don't behave exactly like keys in music. The sequence of tenses, what follows what, is dependent on other factors than the poet's wish to modulate from one to another.

If we look at the first stanza both the imperative and the indicative are in fact a kind of play-acting. The action that is being described is actually in the past. The poet is re-creating the scene, using the 'historic' present to make it vivid and inviting us to share in the experience. We have done so now, our imaginations have been filled with it, and we are ready to let it go. So when the poem closes in the past tense we feel satisfied: the tension between the imperative 'Behold!' and the indicative of statement has been resolved:

> Whate'er the the theme, the Maiden sung
> As if her song could have no ending;
> I saw her singing at her work,
> And o'er the sickle bending;

> I listen'd till I had my fill:
> And, as I mounted up the hill,
> The music in my heart I bore,
> Long after it was heard no more.
> (The earliest text—1807)

Of the three motifs in the first subject, the 'reaping' and the 'singing' are explicitly recapitulated. The fact that she is solitary is taken for granted. Of the two motifs in the second subject, the 'overflowing' quality of the song is clearly present—perhaps unconsciously, the twenty-third psalm ('My cup runneth over') has its place here. But aside from this counting of motifs, I think everyone feels that the poem does in fact come back to its opening, though with the tensions resolved. And that is precisely what the recapitulation in sonata-form is supposed to do.

Wordsworth was an almost exact contemporary of Ludwig von Beethoven, and had something of the same role to play in English poetry as Beethoven played in music. Both reflected acutely the bourgeois aspirations which led to the French Revolution, and the contradictions that the Revolution gave rise to in the world of the spirit. Both tried to work out a synthesis, based on a dialectic of social frustration and personal change of heart, leading to imaginative release. Beethoven's repudiation of his dedication of the third symphony to Napoleon is as much a cultural fact about the Revolution as Wordsworth's slide into undistinguished Toryism. Wordsworth was not so great as Beethoven—there are no last quartets to be found in his poetry but we ought not to be surprised that there are formal parallels between the two masters. Of course, I have cheated: not many of his poems are so close to actual sonata-form as 'The Highland Reaper.' But the formal and entirely symphonic achievements of Wordsworth's great period ('The Idiot Boy,' 'Tintern Abbey,' 'Resolution and Independence' and the 'Ode,' for example) have scarcely been analysed. His achievements in form have hardly been understood at all.*

---

* But see J.F. Danby: *The Simple Wordsworth*, 1960, for a discussion of 'The Idiot Boy.'

Wordsworth's poetry is in itself as much a dialectic process—thesis, antithesis, synthesis—as any symphony of Beethoven. Sonata-form is nothing else but one useful formulation of such a dialectic in musical terms.

To return to myself. In 1959, I had to break out of my strophic stasis as a poet and I felt instinctively that my way lay through the formal principles of late eighteenth-century music. I decided to use sonata-form not accidentally, as Wordsworth did, but with malice aforethought. Now in modern English it is a fact of some significance that every verb form—I go, I might go, I used not to go, I ought to have gone—has a different rhythm to it, and very few of these go into an iambic beat. The English verbs, therefore, whatever they did in Marvell or Wordsworth's day, do not now simply play the part of keys and modes in music: they have a rhythmic function as well, and indeed a melodic one. They are far more like the nature of the scale in Indian music than that in European. Accordingly I decided to build my poem rhythmically as well as structurally out of the resources of the English verb.

'Open Sesame' (from *Metamorphoses*, 1961, revised 1990) was one of the poems that resulted:

OPEN SESAME

You might hear it said in turning lanes,
rock lanes and turning streams,
sheepturns through the shale
and the chipped layers of cloud.

Open the hard ground, chip the slate,　　　　5
let fingers bleed . . .

Perhaps stone might crack, might open
into the longed-for grotto of the night,
and you go down.

And underground streams carry you down　　10
sapphired, infinite passageways,
and you, you must go down
to the innermost cave of all

> broad as a coral sea, and tall
> as a mountain day. There 15
> you might hear it said, Pick up
> the largest gem of all, crack it open
> and enter in. You'd do it,
> and find yourself in turning lanes,
> rock lanes and turning streams, 20
> sheepturns through the shale
> and the chipped layers of cloud.
>
> Weary of charms, you'd walk down
> carefully the narrow paths,
> meet me stumbling down, and come 25
> to the hard little village in the chalice
> of a mere forgivable world.
> And there, lie down.

'Open Sesame' shows the sort of freedom that comes from giving verbs their head. The whole emphasis is on activity and one is not called upon to explain who 'you' is. The obscurity of poems like 'The Ghost' is simply ironed out by the driving force of the verbs. The underlying tensions are expressed through the verbal forms, not allowed to spill over into uncertainties. The rhythm is generated by the opening phrase—'you might hear'—a periphrastic subjunctive that has to be treated with caution in most modern poetry simply because it is difficult to fit into iambic stress. I analyse the poem as follows:

1—4   Exposition of first subject in the subjunctive—'You might hear.'
5—6   Exposition of second subject in the imperative—'Open, chip, let the fingers bleed.'
7—9   Codetta (a little coda), returning to the subjunctive, with an emphatic cadence on 'down.'
10—18 Development section, mostly dependent on 'you might' but glancing at 'you must.'
(15—18 This looks like a recapitulation of the second subject. It is complex because it is in a subordinate clause, for which there is no counterpart in music. The main clause is in the subjunctive, but the actual second subject is still in the

imperative. It is better to regard it as still part of the development.)

18—22 Recapitulation of the first subject, in a different tense— 'You'd do it'—you would do it. As with the Wordsworth poem, one has to remember that tenses and moods of the verb do not work exactly like keys. The tension between the subjunctive and the imperative is in fact resolved by the conditional—'you would do'—not by a return to the subjunctive.

23—28 Coda, again in the conditional. This is based on a new development of lines 5—9, the second subject and the codetta, and serves instead of a straight recapitulation of the second subject. This looks irregular, but is well within the variety of practice found in the classical composers. The point is that the mood of possibility in the first subject and the obsessional striving of the second are reconciled in the going down to 'the hard little village in the chalice of a mere forgivable world.' And there (you would) lie down. Or possibly this verb is ambiguous: the sense could be, 'And there, lie down!'—the imperative having the last word after all!

* * *

Clearly, not many poems can be as directly related to musical form as 'Open Sesame.' Nevertheless the freedom and formal clarity I learnt from such pieces have been invaluable to me. Later on, other features of music—such as inviting the performer to improvise, or giving him tasks which are impossible to perform literally, so that he gets tipped over the edge into creativity—have appealed to me, and some of them I've tried out in the terms of my own art. My friendship in the sixties with Bernard Rands the modernist composer was a great stimulus in these matters. But neither have the major forms of Western music ever lost their challenge for me, as the long poem, *Castles: Variations on an Original Theme*, will show.

THE MUSE

To talk of the Muse, I am told, is either atavistic or precious. And yet (with varying degrees of seriousness) her name still lives in our idioms; and some poets even of this century have claimed she inspired them.

There are several meanings attached to her. On a very general level, for instance, she was a goddess of the compulsion to sing or do trigonometry or tell jokes—or write poems; just as Venus was the goddess of sex or Mars the god of fighting. Whenever your everyday behaviour was superseded by an impersonal force, the Greeks tended to put it down to the activity of a god or goddess. At its most casual, this is a mere question of words. Latin poets refer to 'affairs of Venus' instead of love-affairs or matters of sex. But it also makes possible an acknowledgement of the religious dimension that such a compulsion does indeed have, and at its most intense (say, in a man who has fallen in love or under the bloodlust of battle) qualifies as daemonic possession. The way that a trigonometrical problem, a joke, or the composition of a poem takes you over is more specialised than sex or battle-frenzy, but it is nonetheless real. This kind of 'intellectual' daemon the Greeks tended to allot to the Muses, originally perhaps mountain goddesses with prophetic powers.

In some situations daemonic possession becomes not just an interesting experience but a necessity. If you are fighting a hand-to-hand battle, to get your blood up may be a matter of life and death. Adrenalin level or the help of the god of war—the terms differ, but the experience is no different in ancient Athens from modern Dunkirk. And if you are making love, possession by Venus—the right hormone reaction or whatever—is clearly called for. A jazz musician or a soccer player—like Homer of old—has to be lifted out of himself, or he won't fulfil the expectations of his fans.

Of all these, the job of the epic poet relies most heavily on the Muse's help. And by epic poet, I mean the real article, a man who stands up in the market place or the great hall of a king and recites or 'composes' extempore a long poem that tells a heroic story. Such a poet has, it is true, a wide range of 'epic formulae' and set phrases to help him: it has been shown that practically every half-line in the *Iliad* recurs with minor modifications elsewhere in the poem. Every time we hear it, the poem is unique: no two performances use the formulae in exactly the same way. Indeed the differences may be very large: one rendition may last a mere hour and a half, while another, by the same poet a few days later, may take five or six hours in the telling. Clearly the epic poet, like the jazz musician, relies very heavily on his 'Muse' to see him through. His greatest fear is that he will dry up in the middle of a song. There is a story of one epic poet whose Muse failed him halfway and the audience was so enraged at being left in suspense that they put the wretched fellow to death! That is an extreme case; but we can say that the epic poet's livelihood—his box-office as it were—relies on not drying up too often. He has to have some superhuman power, automatic pilot or Muse to see him through. And whereas the jazz musician or the soccer player are buoyed up by the rest of the band or the other members of the team, the epic poet works by himself, so there is nothing but his talent, his formulae and the trust in his Muse to stand between him and failure.

That is why the metre of epic verse is important. It carries the poet along, it stimulates his subconscious mind, it activates the Muse. And that is also why epic poets frequently start with a set prayer, learnt off by heart, invoking the Muse's help: not only because the poet believes in a personal Muse whose aid can be procured in this way, but also for a technical reason, because the reciting of the set prayer acts as a stimulant and starts up the all-important rhythm in his subconsious.

Those two uses of 'Muse', in Greek mythology and in epic, are easy to put into words. The third is more difficult. In some sense or other we recognise that a poet may respond to a woman so that he is inspired to write poetry qualitatively different to what he wrote before. The experience is often called 'falling in love'– Catullus fell in love with Lesbia, Dante with Beatrice, Keats with Fanny Brawne; but in fact it often carries with it a strongly a-sexual or even anti-sexual element. Catullus' greatest poem is a wildly passionate description of a devotee of the Goddess Cybele castrating himself in a frenzy of religious ecstasy. Dante never touched Beatrice, but worshipped her without her knowledge, so it seems, until her early death. Even Keats at the end could hardly bear to be in the same room as Fanny, she affected him so much he was too ill to stand it.

> La Belle Dame Sans Merci
> Hath me in thrall.

So the term 'falling in love' is not usually accurate. Poets and their muses, it would seem, do not often form successful marriages.

Thomas Hardy is interesting in this connexion, because he wrote his greatest love-poetry to his first wife's ghost. His marriage to her, not a very happy one, had to be got out of the way before she could enter her real relationship with him as a Muse. In fact Muses are quite often dead by the time they inspire their poets to greatness. The prime example is of course Beatrice. Dante did not start to write the *Divine Comedy* until about ten years after her death.

It often seems that the Muse's relation to her poet is more like mother to son than one between equal and adult lovers. When Dante finally meets Beatrice again in the earthly Paradise of the *Purgatorio*, she scolds him like a schoolboy, even though part of her indictment is that he is old enough to have known better:

> As a mother may seem stern to her child
> So she appeared to me; because it is a bitter
> Taste that is left by sharpness in pity . . .

The Muse is triune, according to Robert Graves: maiden, mother and hag. But her chief function for the poet is as a guide. For Hardy, the ghost leads him back to his memories of their early love. For Keats, in the *Hyperion* fragments, Moneta shows him the despair of the Titans and the new kind of divinity that is to be. For Coleridge, the Abyssinian maid's song, if he could revive it within him, would enable him to rebuild the vision of Kubla Khan's pleasure dome. And of course, Beatrice leads Dante through Hell, Purgatory and Heaven, either in person or with the aid of Virgil.

The specific form that the relationship between Muse and poet takes is very varied, and often lends itself to mythological treatment. But it is not in itself a myth. The girl is usually real enough; or if she is not, but merely some imaginary being, that fact usually limits her effectiveness as a guide. Dylan Thomas's later poetry seems haunted by a Muse who never quite becomes real—the imagined girl of the 'Hunchback in the Park' or 'A Winter's Tale', or the girl used as a bait for all the sea-creatures in 'The Ballad of the Long-legged Bait'. Her guidance is incoherent and the poet is left stranded in the never-never land of his childhood, a generalised past of 'Country Sleep'.

There are two main theoretical systems on the market which offer to explain the Muse, those of Robert Graves and Carl Jung respectively. That of Robert Graves is based on his own experience as a poet of the formidable Muse, Laura Riding, a poet herself and one who deliberately gave up poetry when she left him; and of several other Muses subsequent to her going. (It is common for poets, when the one Muse leaves them, to find surrogates for her. It happened to Dante also.) Graves offers essentially a religious explanation. The Muse is the primordial Goddess, the Earth-mother, who was worshipped by neolithic farmers all the world over. The ancient tribal kings derived their power and their immortality from her, both as her sons and as her lovers. They were also her victims, sacrificed to her for the good of the crops. In some never quite explained way, true poets are descended from her shaman-like priests. They keep to her worship though the rest of mankind has forsaken her for the usurping male deities—Zeus, Apollo or Jehovah. The Goddess continuously inspires a religious fifth column, who keep her values alive in a naughty world. True poetry, which can only be composed under her love and inspiration, is an embodiment of her truth. Particular Muses, like Beatrice or Fanny or Laura Riding, incarnate for the poet the One Goddess herself, in all her fascinating variety.

Jung's version is a trifle more secular, part of his general theory of archetypes of the Collective Unconscious. Roughly speaking, he posits a female element in every man (the anima) and a male element in every woman (the animus). It is with the anima that we are now concerned:

> An inherited collective image of woman exists in a man's unconscious, with the help of which he can apprehend the nature of women.

This image only becomes tangible through the actual contacts he makes with women, such as his mother or his girl-friends, and is projected onto them. The anima is both young and wise, fascinating and beautiful, comforting and dangerous. She is often very powerful and disturbing, and has a sense of secret meaningfulness about her. Sometimes she is good, but for other men she can be terrible, a hag who pursues them remorselessly. Her appearances are inconsistent with each other, yet always recognisable. A man possessed by his anima is a prey to uncontrollable emotion. Frieda Fordham, in her Pelican on Jung, says:

> Both the animus and the anima are mediators between the conscious and the unconscious mind, and when they become personified in fantasies, dreams or visions they present an opportunity to understand something of what has hitherto been subconscious.

Both these theories seem to be pretty shaky constructions but each of them can be useful, on the level of what Keats called 'notions'. They can give you tools to understand and chart what is happening to you in the experience of loving a Muse.

One of the surprising things about Welsh poetry is its lack of Muses. True, in the mythology connected with Taliesin, there is a story about Ceridwen and her cauldron of inspiration. Ceridwen prepared a magic potion in this cauldron to give to her son Morfran; but little Gwion, who was guarding the cauldron for her, by accident tasted it first; whereupon she gave chase and at last swallowed him; he was reborn as her child, the poet Taliesin. Undoubtedly Ceridwen is the Muse, but Gwion is not her chosen poet. Gwion obtains inspiration by an accident that is a sort of cheating; and once Taliesin is born, Ceridwen the Muse plays no further part in the story. In the *Four Branches*, also, male magicians are portrayed as outwitting crypto-Goddess figures like Arianrhod and Blodeuwedd.

On the whole Welsh poetry is a very masculine affair. The *awen* or Muse is hardly ever personalised as a woman, as far as I know. Of course there are plenty of poems to girls, from Dafydd ap Gwilym downwards, and one would not want to be dogmatic about them all; but in what I have read, the women remain just sweethearts, wives or would-be sexual objects, or the wives or daughters of patrons. None of them change the style of the poetry, none of them act as guides, none of them mediate between the conscious and the subconscious mind. However much the *awen* uses the subconscious in order to create poetry, Welsh poets in general write for conscious and socially useful ends. The Welsh tradition is a tradition of light not darkness, consciousness not dream or vision or the archetypes of myth.

In this century, I am not sure. In some respects, Wales herself, or the Welsh language, is often portrayed as a sort of anima-figure, and typically she has two aspects, light and dark, princess and prostitute, virgin and hag. This development is typical of a culture in crisis: one thinks of the lamenting women who represent Ireland in the *aislings* of eighteenth-century poets like Aoga(n) Ó Rathaille (Egan O'Rahilly). In Waldo Williams, the Welsh language clearly functions as a Muse, bringing him hope and mediating between the conscious mind and the subconscious strength of the tradition:

> And she is danger's daughter. Her path the wind whips,
> Her feet where they tired, where they fell, those of the lower air.
> Till now she has seen her way clearer than prophets.
> She is as young as ever, as full of mischief.
> ('Cymru a Chymraeg')

As for more personal Muses, one thinks again of Waldo Williams and his wife, Linda, who died only a year after their marriage. Only two poems in *Dail Pren*—his solitary book of poems, 'Leaves of a Tree', a quotation from Keats—are actually about Linda, but his acknowledgement of her importance as a guide and a '*cydymdaith*' (one who goes on a journey with you) is not in doubt: both his poems to Linda are richly metaphorical, major poems and revolutionary within their tradition. This is not the place to elucidate their difficulties, but here is the shorter of them, '*Oherwydd Ein Dyfod*,' in my own translation:

BECAUSE OF OUR COMING

Because of our coming into the quiet room,
In the timeless cavern,
And because of our going out
Into the network of roots
And into orchards of apples,

And because of our going out
Through the dark veins
Into the light of bright hearths
And me, because of my following
The warm heart,
My night star,
My secret of day . . .

And a kiss out to every star restoring
The deep ocean, the archipelago,
And two breasts making a new earth,
Two arms sheltering the country . . .

Because of our coming to the house built strong
With peace its foundation
For the joy of our love,

And the world itself coming
To the deep happiness
Within sound of the footfall
Of my gold girl.

One notices the twofold journey through darkness and light—into the network of roots and the apple orchards, and through the dark veins into the light of bright hearths. Waldo follows the warm heart, 'my night star, my secret of day': '*seren fy nos a rhin fy nydd.*' '*Rhin*' is a wider word than 'secret'—it can mean something like 'virtue'. One is reminded of Bethlehem, surely. Linda is the star leading him. In the next lines she becomes almost like God, renewing the whole world, her arms sheltering the countryside ('*bro*', one's native region, that word so difficult to translate). And at the end the world itself comes to the two of them, to 'within sound of the footfall / Of my gold girl'. He suddenly uses a word that generations of love-poets had used before him, '*eurferch*',' gold girl', as if to connect his vision with all the love poets of Wales, right back to Dafydd ap Gwilym and beyond. I find that '*eurferch*' perhaps the most surprising word in the whole poem. In terms of register it seems so different from the rest of the diction, and yet it is absolutely right, the gold picking up both the star and the secret, both Bethlehem and the light of bright hearths.

Darkness and light, dream and everyday reality, night star and secret of day: these are the familiar dichotomies of the Muse. I would like now to offer some observations on my own experience. From 1959 till 1966 or 7, from when I was twenty-seven until I was thirty-five or six, my poetry was written to a girl called Liz, and then, after she left in 1960, to whatever girls could momentarily fill her role, culminating in an American called Judy. I have told the story, such as it is, in the Introduction to my *Poems, 1951-67*, so there is no need to give a blow by blow account. Up to the time I met Liz, my poetry had been swanning around, without much sense of purpose. I had found no poetic country that was mine.

I had already written some verses to Liz before she revealed herself as a Muse to me, in two tiny poems that I promptly forgot I'd written. I found them weeks later in a notebook, and remembered when I looked at the notes that I had been sitting next to her in the library. Here is the first of them:

SIGNET RING

I hold in my squat round
By a mere fingerful
A whole world,

> A redemption,
> A brave claim.
> What's more, I give
> That majesty
> A name.

I made my claim on her shortly after that, when she wrote a poem to me and I to her. There was a certain degree of mutuality in our relationship, and a great deal of affection; but she was never my mistress. I was totally obsessed with her for years afterwards, and her power over me was at once deathlike and intensely stimulating. During the less than two years when she came to me often as a Muse, I wrote over two dozen poems, one of them over four hundred lines long.

A great many of these are love poems, calling out to her to come to me, to let me into her darkness. Others are narratives, in which I gave her dreams. I mean that quite literally. It seemed to me that she needed to be healed of some great psychological wound, and I had great faith in the healing power of dreams. Some years before, I had been converted to Christianity because of a dream. Actually, looking back, it was probably my own psychological wound that the dreams had to heal. I shall say more about that in a moment. Such was my conceit and innocence that in order to find what I needed in her darkness, I had to believe I was finding it for her. But I am not certain about this,—it is quite a long time ago, and I may have intuited something real about her too.

Waldo talks about 'our going out / Through the dark veins / Into the light of bright hearths.' I do not know what these words meant to him, but to me they are a precise description of what happened when I wrote poems to Liz. Let me contrast the situation with the general run of poetry writing. A poet may get an idea, which he holds in a semi-conscious way over a period of days or weeks or even years. He may worry at it at intervals, and gradually certain rhythmic features, certain ways of looking at it, certain phrases or actual lines, may condense around the initial idea or stimulus—whatever it is. At a certain point he starts to write the poem. He may take it through many drafts, correcting and shaping it on the page. That is the way a lot of poets work: most of the time, that is, they are operating 'at the back of their consciousness,' in daylight, as it were. They work at something whose subject matter is known to them—very often, these days, at a past experience they may have had. Like any writer they try to get the experience down on the page.

I have not often worked like this, until very recently. The ways in which I write poetry have been quite varied, but they almost all involve speed. There is just no time for the long process of accretion, like a pearl growing in an oyster. Always I try to involve the arbitrary, the unorganic thisness that is turned up by the present moment. My poems are essentially dances round what is presented to me at the moment of creation. Of course, they will use memory, thought, emotion that is old—maybe lifetimes old. But I do not know, except sometimes in very general terms, what my subject matter is going to be, if indeed there is going to be one. I like to travel light in these matters.

Let me describe a typical experience—what happened when I wrote a poem in the days when I had a Muse. A poem to Liz. Of course, you have to remember that this is a story. During the actual creation of a work of art, you have other things to do than make precise observations of what is going on. But it is a story that may point in the right direction. It is, anyway, the best I can do.

For perhaps a day or two before a poem, I got more and more grumpy and impossible to be with. Usually I took every direction but that to my typewriter. I wandered round the place feeling haunted and irritable. Then, usually last thing at night, when I was dog-tired, sometimes so tired I was choking with it, it cornered me. I would often kneel with my head in an armchair, going down, down, down. Sometimes I would make desultory prayers more to give my consciousness something to do, like Alice looking at the various shelves on her way down the rabbit hole, than for any religious reason. The darkness was the religious thing, not any prayers I might make to a largely irrelevant deity. I never, of course, prayed to Liz.

Suddenly I was sitting in front of a typewriter with a clean sheet of paper in it, typing. Words would wash over me, all kinds of words, beautiful, ugly words, They were irrelevant, but some of them I usually managed to write down. Then a phrase, or a line or two, would come that had power. Liz was all round me, I was talking to her. The poem was there. After that, it was more like delivering a baby than anything else. Pulling it out whole. Sometimes, for a minute or two, the tension would break and I would surface, light a cigarette or walk round the room. Then back again, into the darkness.

It was like delivering a baby. It was like intimate love-making talk. It was like dancing. It was the most concentrated work I have ever done. In something like three quarters of an hour the thing ran into the sand. I realised I was not getting anywhere. Had it all been for nothing? Then I saw that maybe twenty lines back the real poem had finished. What I was dealing with now was just afterbirth. In savage joy I recognised my child, my poem come into the light of day.

If you had asked me then what the poem was about, it is likely that I would not have known.

That is the story. I do not know how accurate it is, or how much it accords with other poets' experience. As I say, the manifestations of the Muse are very varied; and no two Muses are alike.

When it comes to the poems that are composed in this way, or in similar darkness, how to judge them, how to talk about them, I am up against a difficulty. On the whole, my poems to Liz have not received much recognition. I am haunted by a joke I once heard about Shakespere being asked which of his plays he liked best. The bard stroked his beard and said, rather shyly, 'Well, you know, I always thought *Titus Adronicus* had something rather special about it.' Are these Muse-poems my *Titus Adronicus*? But then I look at the contemporary poetic climate and reflect on how secular it is, how devoted to 'creative writing,' and in Wales how dominated by the teaching profession, and really I'm not sure. Post-war English poetry is largely devoted to consciousness, to style, to making the best use of one's material. Imagism is its chosen method. The English have turned thankfully away from Freud and Jung, back to the empiricism where they feel safe. And the Welsh have not had much truck with Muses for a good few centuries. The language of dreams that the Muse speaks as of right has few *dysgwyr* among the critics.

It seems to me worthwhile to show you a few of these dances from the Muse-darkness. They are not well known, and in any case since their publication I have extensively revised them. I will begin with an early poem to Liz, soon after I 'claimed' her:

ONE MORNING

As you walked out one morning in the cold
You shrank to the size of a sixpenny bit
Alone in a jungle of grasses.

Your tiny ghost came out to kill
Its corporal imprisoner.
Over the pollen-tarnished mud
The little phantom tracked you down
As you walked out in the cold.

Now you were small (thought that small ghost)
You'd be amenable to death.
A drop of dew could drown
Or an ant's sting drop you down
And stifle that poor breath.

As you fled from your ghost,
Whimpering in the cold,
Crying like a gnat from fear
And hiding away
In a dead snail or hollow stalk,
Whimpering and timid to your ghost,
Tried in the pits for death,
In the eyes, nostrils, closed teeth, ears,
In the navel and the loins
For the incoming of death;
As you melted and fried and burnt,
Drowned, drowned and gasped for breath,
Pricked like a witch for the mark of your dying,
Now you were small and serviceable to death . . .

> The sun rose. One morning in the cold
> You walked out of your smallness.
> And it was so. The sun shone down
> And it was Easter. Jesus talked in the trees,
> Mary and the company of angels
> Were gold like buttercups.
> As you walked out one morning your ghost died.
> It was day, the City beneath you
> Tingled with light. The slates of the City
> Greeted you, comforted you
> As you walked home one morning in the sun.

I hope you can see how this is a dance. It almost asks to be choreographed with its strong, rhythmic beat and the constant use of language as gesture—'greeted you, comforted you.' The way it tells its fairytale story is essentially balletic.

What is the dance doing? Surely it is creating some kind of waking dream, at first a nightmare of being totally small and defenceless, then of finding yourself the right size again. I am sure it does different things for different people. I used to think it was about 'feeling small' in the sense of being ashamed or inadequate. But taken with other poems from those years, I now realise it is probably a dream of birth. The common factor is a sense of expectant dreariness or fear, a nightmare of futility and a longing to escape. The escape, when it comes, is into a tired but happy fulfilment; but sometimes it never comes at all and the futility is unending.

Be that as it may, the poem does not *mean* that. Its subject matter is what it says it is, a fantasy about being small and vulnerable. What you make of the fantasy is really up to you. I would say, however, that these are serious poems, they can carry weight. Read properly, they challenge many of our preconceptions. They take seriously, for example, the values of innocence. They travel light. Here is a love-poem to Liz which dances the holy folly of not binding to yourself a joy:

CHRISTMAS IS COMING

My dear one, if I could give away desire
as easily and cheaply as a ten bob note
and leave Time happy at my tip, and leave
time happy just to stroll the roads,
the lanes where vetches tangle, utterly absorbed
in my happiness in you—

if I could only
take even my happiness in you, and throw it
like a sixpence in a fountain, and not bother
even to wish—

oh if I could only
chuck up my you-found bliss, or keep it
in a breast pocket like a farthing, not for use
but as a charm or talisman for nothing
or for you, my dear one, nothing

                        or God bless you—

both—

              for keeps—

    The dance here is more one of paradox than of physical gesture, but even so the verbs suggest the gestures of mime—*give away, leave* [someone] *happy at my tip, stroll, throw it like a sixpence in a fountain, chuck up, keep it in a breast pocket*. The way the puns turn phrases inside out—*leave Time happy at my tip* and *leave time happy just to stroll*—also seems choreographic to me.

    I could obviously go on pulling poems out of the hat for a long time. I do not understand how such things could have given Jeremy Hooker, for example, the initial impression that I was a late Romantic. They seem to me as modernist as anything I've ever done, and as sceptical of mythologies.

    As a sort of summing-up, here is a poem I wrote (not to Liz) using the image of the prehistoric cave-painters at Lascaux to 'dance' what happened in the muse-darkness when I wrote the kind of poetry that I have been describing. The theory is that these paintings were done as imitative magic. Just as the deer, bison, cattle etc. appeared on the walls of the sacred cave, so they would appear in reality on the grasslands above; and thus the skill of the painter summoned the great herds so that the skill of the hunter could feed the tribe.

I DANCE WITHIN THE FOSSIL ROOT

I insert my two eyes,
Down
This upward budding
Contorted
Stem of the world; and

(Trading delusionary gems
That the rushlight scatters
To chunnering black ghosts)

Stamp dances on the doom-root
To snare
In the carnivorous
Flower
Opening above me
Masterful ungulates...

And the root after many crimson
Deaths lets the cold chalk
Document my barter

GIRL WEEPING / HERMES

The Story of a Poem

As I have explained in the last chapter, at the time I wrote the poems in *Metamorphoses* I was very much drawn into the darkness of a girl called Liz. Her lover had just left her, to return to a long-standing engagement. Though he married someone else it was clear he still loved her. She was left insecure and dangerous. She seemed to run through men, mauling their self-esteem like a fire through gorse. She became my muse. I wrote poems to her, to give her the dreams of healing that she needed. She did not understand, but she came to me, and in her darkness I made the poems.

One day late in autumn her lover came back. He took Liz out to the castle at Beaumaris, on the Menai Straits. He stayed with me that night and we talked. It was five o'clock before we went to bed. At seven I got up, made myself a coffee and wrote 'Hermes' in six three-line stanzas. When I had finished it, in conditions not far from waking dream, I woke my friend to show him the new poem that had been born.

The poem is a dream I give to Liz. I look into her tears as she is crying over her predicament. They seem like a landscape—the landscape of the Menai Straits looking over to Beaumaris, or the landscape of the Styx, the river of death. The two scenes mingle and enrich each other throughout the poem. My friend and her lover appears first as Hermes, the trim and naked god who leads the dead down to Hades—Hermes Psychopompos, the leader of souls. If she follows him, she is surely a ghost. But Hermes though he is all-powerful on this river, and the eyes of the fortress command her dream, nevertheless allows a more ancient dispensation, the life of her womanhood, represented by the two herons. 'Their life ignores his force.' They sanctify her tears, making them honourable and human. It is right to weep for impossible love, to pity oneself bereaved, to suffer as we escape unreality and waste.

To say that my friend, her lover, appears in the poem as Hermes is only partly true. Hermes is not my friend: he is the god of merchants and markets, the god of capitalism, the god of robbers, the messenger of the gods; as well as the guide of the dead. From my friend's point of view—for the dream could just as well be addressed to him as to Liz (or even to me, we were all suffering!)—Hermes could well have been the effect Liz was having on him, rather than the other way round. Hermes stands perhaps for the socialization of the death-wish; for all neat and tidy final solutions to the pain of being alive.

The poem could very well be interpreted in a Marxist way, as a contrast between the power of capitalism (Hermes) allied to feudal-fascist militarism (the fortress), and the still continuing life of humanity, the rags and tatters of lost tribal community (the herons) prophesying the new life.

Like all dreams the poem is quite simple to experience. It is only the explication that becomes complicated and difficult. I do not claim that the personal significance it had for the three of us should be the paramount meaning it should have for anyone else. When it was first written, it had six stanzas. But the second stanza seemed so private—the reference to Beaumaris hardly seemed necessary for the public poem—that I left it out when I published it in *Metamorphoses* 1961. In the version that follows I restore it as it was first written in Autumn 1959, preserved in the fair copy I gave to my friend early that morning. (One other change I have made since: the title is now not 'Hermes' but 'Girl Weeping / Hermes': it sounds enigmatic but it does give the reader a better clue to begin with).

I should perhaps add that I had seen two herons by the Straits the day before; and that herons have always been for me birds of good omen. I compare them to 'Simeons,' a reference to Luke, 2, 25-36:

> And, behold, there was a man in Jerusalem, whose name was Simeon; and the same man was just and devout, waiting for the consolation of Israel: and the Holy Ghost was upon him. And it was revealed unto him by the Holy Ghost, that he should not see death, before he had seen the Lord's Christ. And he came by the

Spirit into the temple: and when the parents brought in the child Jesus, to do for him after the custom of the law, then he took him up in his arms, and blessed God, and said, 'Lord, now lettest thou thy servant depart in peace, according to thy word: for mine eyes have seen thy salvation, which thou hast prepared before the face of all people; a light to lighten the Gentiles, and the glory of thy people Israel.'

And Joseph and his mother marvelled at those things which were spoken of him. And Simeon blessed them, and said unto Mary his mother, 'Behold, this child is set for the fall and rising again of many in Israel; and for a sign which shall be spoken against; (Yea, a sword shall pierce through thy own soul also) that the thoughts of many hearts may be revealed.'

Most of the associations of the above passage, full of Luke's characteristic humanity, mixing great peace with past and future suffering, are relevant to the feeling in my poem.

HERMES

Is mercy flowering in the lands of the dead
as over the river the winged feet walk
in the auburn dusk of your tears?

The squat grey fortress on the bank
hidden in alder, is like a toad
whose staring eyes command your dream.

The trim and naked god, whose company
all ghosts find grateful, touches
hardly at all the golden foam he walks.

I watch two herons with stretched legs
and necks bent like a tripod, wheel
on the rags of their rectangular wings.

They are so old, and such impoverished
Simeons, that the brisk god of robbers
permits them to inhabit this near death.

Their life ignores his force. They fly
like dowagers of a once lovely epoch
giving bright honour to such childish tears.

THE WORLD AS ASYMPTOTE

The poems to Liz in *Metamorphoses* had ended in a mood of joy, in songs of innocence, even if, in 'Other than we,' the joy was precarious and the innocence only preserved by distinguishing the real 'we' from 'our warring wits' and 'a loneliness stolen from two.' In *Asymptotes*,* written after Liz had left Bangor, the poems became increasingly disconsolate. It was not simply that I felt miserable without her. As far as I remember, that was not particularly the case, at least on the surface. But my poetry felt lost. The subjunctive, which in the Lizbook had been the activator of so much realizable possibility, now became a mood of doubt and an infinite regress of mirrors. 'Asymptote' is a metaphor from co-ordinate geometry, a line that approaches nearer and nearer to a given curve but does not meet it within a finite distance. 'Suppose' is typical of the series. The title has to be read as part of the first line:

SUPPOSE

In an afternoon's careless walk, you turn
like a dancestep without thought
down the unusual path—so light the air,
so near the safe road home—and suddenly
(suppose) stop being you

And then this knowledge
be for a few moments accepted,
grasped in the mind—before it bite,
stun you like the shocked terror
of only five more ticking hours to live:
madness, groping in the abyss
for the one comfort of a memory

---

* '*Metamorphoses*, *Asymptotes* and *Stelae* in this and the following essays do not refer to the separate pamphlets of those names, but to sections of *Collected Lyrics 1950-90* (col. 1991).

> But in those previous moments—what?
> Suppose you're singing an air,
> loving a man, a great musician,
> a mystic at the brink
> of Godhead
>
> Or suppose
> like a dancestep without thought, you're turning
> down the unusual path—so light the air,
> so near the safe road home—and suddenly
> (suppose) coming to where
> the not you has its ending, almost you again . . .

The poem is an analysis of madness, of going mad. Insanity was only one possibility out of many in the flux of losing your 'youness,' your identity as a person. You might have found the way back, or you might have discovered a new self, infinitely richer than the one you'd lost. But terror blocked you doing that, and so you are now fixed in madness.

Technically it is very close to the poems in the Lizbook that are based on musical structures such as sonata-form. Like 'Open Sesame,' it is built on the rhythms of the verb:

> 'suppose you turn'
> 'suppose you're singing'

These virtual subjunctives dominate the whole poem: the contrast between the past definite and the imperfect is what describes the asymptote.

The poems arise from the suddenness and unpredictability of experience, the evanescence of happiness, and the loss or absence of a stable self. The 'unnaming' is not always painful or negative. Happiness, for instance, in the poem of that name –

> I did not find the plant, no, not for all my searching
> until a smile of yours led me to common ground . . .
>
> And now, wherever I look, so blind was I before,
> I see it common as bindweed, everywhere

> a constant, lazy tune, like a brook or kettle
> as generally unnoticed as a piece of sky.

But more often the possibility of happiness is on the road you cannot take, as in 'Three Seeds':

> And in my dream
> you said, 'I found this flower
> in a valley I may not walk . . .'

Even our own past has become asymptotic to us. While we are in the seaport town of 'The Harbour' the strangeness is acceptable and 'timely true'; but what happens when we leave?

> Anonymous, all enter the whitewashed town
> for till you leave this seaport
> all's timely true, nothing is unforeseen.
> A legend has it that this town, called Cana,
> was where Adam first saw Eve. Therefore no trouble
> of being alone vexes the heart's unnaming
> of what was known and now is strange as childhood
> for ever transfixed in the harsh yelp of gulls.

Technically, in the Lizbook I had found clarity by concentrating on the verb, which had given me the freedom to articulate mental processes without getting bogged down in the circumstances and nature of the agent. That clarity and freedom had now lost itself in an asymptotic world of doubt and uncertainty. The lost nouns, the agents 'unnamed,' seemed to be taking their revenge. Once again, I had to find a new way to organise a poem which would not land me in a no-man's-land.

THE PAINTER'S HAND

One day in 1961 I opened the door of Powys hall in the college and found myself in an exhibition of paintings. They were oils, quite small, mostly in browns and greys, landscapes and still lifes that clearly derived from the Gwynedd post-industrial scene of ruined slate-mills and deserted quarries. Very few of the objects were obvious—these were hardly representational pictures. Some were like guardians, gaunt shapes looming over dark hillsides. Others seemed inspired by the debris of rusted machines. Most of them were lit by moonlight, and in many the moon herself, a rounded square of white or grey, dominated the composition. Like many paintings of the time they had an old-master sort of finish. They were clearly *made* objects with frames that had been designed in three dimensions from wood and margins of canvas as part of the effect. You looked through the framing as if through an arrow-slit in a castle.

The artist was Victor Neep. We made friends. He was selling his pictures absurdly cheaply, and I bought one for ten pounds—the first painting I ever owned. It was called 'Interior' and it was dominated by draperies over a chair. There were hints of a monarch on a throne, and much of the texture of the upper part reminded you of bone.

As I looked at it I became aware that it was not just a visual object, but a dance. It had been built up layer by layer, and over most of the surface the brush-strokes were careful and unobtrusive, dwelling on the textures. It was a very tactile experience, looking at it. The rich softness of the drapery contrasted with the warm hardness of the chair wood and the striated white bone. It was more richly coloured than most of his paintings: although the basic contrasts were different shades of brown and luminous white, there was a large purple-blue rounded square at the back of the seat, and a brilliant fold of dark red velvet (as it were) just below it. It was this red that gave me the clue to the dance, for it had been executed in just one large brush-stroke, a flattened S of red paint quite different from most of the

'Interior' by Victor Neep

picture. I then saw that right at the bottom there was another such large brushstroke, a kind of white skid-mark that seemed to want to slide the bottom of the chair along the folds of the drapery away to the right. The whole composition was in fact swinging (or trying to swing) like a bell from the bone-like rounded triangle where the seater's head was suggested.

I say, trying to swing, for the picture was not unstabilized in spite of this powerful rotatory movement. The tension held. The chair did not fall over. After a minute or two experimenting by covering up bits of the painting with my hand, I discovered that it was held in place by a small white rectangle of light reflected on the top right corner of the chair back. Without that to pin it in place the whole picture skidded.

It was a revelation to me. Previously I had only *looked* at paintings. Now I was coming to realise that essentially a painting is a dance, a muscular control of the brush comparable to the conductor's dance with his baton. Was there anything in poetry that could make words dance like that?

First of all I tried to make paintings in words. 'Virgin of the Cave,' for instance, takes the theme of two Leonardo da Vinci pictures, one in London and one in the Louvre, gets rid of the infant John the Baptist and the angel, and transposes the whole thing into a cubist variation, possibly to be painted by Victor Neep:

VIRGIN OF THE CAVE

The stillness of this cavern
is pain's prime axis, pole star's
occluded distance. Frontstage,
a wimple and a fluted cavity
in monochrome.

In the trilling of a bird
dawn lengthens, hovers
onto rock, onto white wimple

that looks to the limp of strata,
gazes out, foresuffering the grief

> of the lank boy
> whose coming the bird sings.
> (1962, rev. 1991)

The Madonna is reduced to a wimple, though her womb may also be suggested by the 'fluted cavity in monochrome.' The cavern is the place where Christ is born, and therefore its stillness is the axis of pain—an axis is a line around which a curve can be rotated symmetrically, for example, the diameter of a circle or the line through the two focuses of an ellipse. The earth rotates on its north-south axis every day. The pole star is roughly on this axis continued into outer space. So, if pain's axis runs through this cavern, the distance from its 'pole star' Godhead—is 'occluded'— shut, closed, or absorbed, by the incarnation. I dare say that it is not necessary to explore the geometrical implications of the metaphor too closely—an impressionistic sense of what it means is all that you need, and most people will have that.

The poem is built on the tension between the dawn lengthening into the cave and the white wimple (the Virgin) looking out. She looks 'to the limp of strata' the generations in the rock limping towards this moment, but also a visual picture of the contortions of rock that she sees. Her gaze 'foresuffers' the grief of her son, the 'lank boy whose coming the bird sings.' He is both the sufferer of grief and the hope of the new dawn.

I found this new technique difficult to control, which is why my revision of the poem is drastic. There was a constant temptation to confuse the basic structure with irrelevant details. The intellectual clutter of my mind tended to make what in any case was quite difficult downright obscure. In order to give the style a chance, I had to free it from theology.

'Virgin of the Cave' is almost a private poem, in the sense that I had no great hopes that other people would find it as stimulating as I did. Victor Neep once showed me a tiny dark square picture which he said was the seed of all he had ever done since. He kept it by him as an inspiration and a talisman. 'Virgin of the Cave' had something of that talismanic function for me.

In two poems I tried to deal with the phenomenon of Neep directly. I bought several of his paintings over the next few years, and some he gave me. One I was very fond of was a portrait of his daughter as a little girl. He used to paint at night, in the kitchen of his house in Bethesda. Sometimes Katie would come down when she couldn't sleep or had nightmares. She would sit watching him paint until she was sleepy enough to go back to bed. He painted several 'night-portraits' of her, with big dark eyes.

VICTOR NEEP PAINTS HIS DAUGHTER KATIE

> Towers congeal in a twinkle. Engineers
> concoct their aqueducts to spider a land
> with silver, hooked at the beck of a moon.
> Out of grey dreams Katie comes down to him.
>
> The eyes ringed wide with a black sleep,
> dark hair dropped to the nightdress of a child
> fleeced slender at the neck . . . she sits so still,
> all the night long it seems, so uncomplaining.
>
> The tenderness of his contemplation
> clears space for her from nightmare
> in a few staccato, gentle words
> that bob like a wagtail, or a dowser's twig.
>
> Tick tock, go minutes. Into the night
> his portrait of her settles
> to the reaching utterance of his brush
> like ripples patterning a wave.

The painter's dance is interrupted by the girl, who then, without losing her loved uniqueness, becomes herself the focus of the dance. This situation, too, was a paradigm of how I wanted my art to function in the human world. I wanted the visitor from Porlock to be made welcome in Xanadu, and to have Kubla Khan's pleasure domes personalised for his use.*

---

* Coleridge's note to 'Kubla Khan' claims that he wrote the poem in a dream, which he started to write down when he awoke; but a visitor from Porlock interrupted him, so that the poem remains a fragment of what was originally in his mind.

The other poem was more simply an attempt to transfer the effect of a painting into verbal terms.

'FIGURE ON A HILLSIDE'

painting by Victor Neep

This on the hill
is of a lost tribe. No one
now knows what brought it, but it stands
scanning by whim the counties under it,

perhaps deciphers
the narrowing cries of bats,
the earth-codes of the mole; or else
spanners the blank moon through its slot of stars.

Godsend of murk
it dies into the landscape like a plough,
endures beyond suffering, impersonal gaunt shape,
Twentieth Century man's best image of himself,

watchful and silent,
hollowed by the wind, towering
in an October dawn
over brown badger ground and pleading roots.

1962, rev. 1989

Vic used to say that painters criticised his paintings because they were too like sculptures, and sculptors disliked his sculptures because they were too like paintings! He had studied with Henry Moore as well as Ceri Richards. Certainly 'Figure on a Hillside'—the second picture of his that I bought—could have been a painting of a sculpture, but I never objected to it on those grounds: as a painting it still seems marvellous to me, a mysterious guardian emerging from nightmare into the human dawn. And yet it is also a dead machine, a ruined gantry. When I first wrote the poem it began like this:

> Machines have graveyards: across torn acres
> disembowelled lorries
> hang with a dead grin over black gaps of rust.
> Between the corpses, mournful willowherb
> and sour nettles grow. But dead machines
> are best found solitary, frozen
> like mammoths in ten-acre fields,
> dignified spare parts
> in a thorn hedge. Iron subsides,
> becomes soil, part of the world. Subtle engines
> soon fidgit into rust. Ivy spells it out.

I came to the conclusion, though, that this was a different poem, whether complete or a fragment I have never decided.

In subsequent pieces I used this pictorial technique more or less consciously to organise what I wanted to say. Here is an example. The title is meant to suggest Vermeer:

> GIRL BY A WINDOW
>
> The sun has come from greenland
> to kneel down
> in the stable of your collar bone.
>
> From the Isle of Man
> tugged naughtily by wet
> he kneels. He stirs the gold chaff
> under the draught of his knee.
>
> The slight movement creates silence.
>
> . . . And from Ireland once, swung down shrouds
> of monkeying rain, tragic winds
> homed my lord Essex to his Queen.
>
> Her old and freckled fingers did not a moment
> cease toying with her meditative orb.
> They were to write his death. The blown sun

>   kneels in a far corner of your flesh,
>   wiser than earls or lovers, surreptitious
>   and impersonal as a night-watchman's cry.
>
> 1963

Vermeer's girls look out of windows, they play harpsichords, they read letters, or pour milk, or listen to young men making polite conversation. The moment is never explicit in its demands on them. It seems to last for ever in a potency that suffuses them like sunlight. And yet one knows, and the painting never denies it, that they will fall in love, suffer, be raped, be great ladies, drudge all their lives, teach children. Yet the moment of sunlight, of waiting, of homage, still keeps its absolute integrity.

In my poem the sun has come from 'greenland' (*sic*), from the 'Isle of Man.' Since the poem was written in north Wales, these are very unlikely places for the sun to come from! It is the sort of day when a cold front has just passed and the sun is coming out behind the subsiding wind and rain. The sun is male, he is tugged naughtily by wet, he kneels (like one of the Magi) in the stable, but not of Bethlehem—'in the stable of your collar bone.' The sexuality of the sun in the poem is matched by his discretion—'the slight movement creates silence.'

Musically, the poem is in classical binary form: the first section or theme in one key is followed by a second section which opens in another (usually related) key but finally moves back into the first. The two simple tenses, present and past, fill the role of the two musical keys. The second section alludes to the story of the earl of Essex's fall and death. He was a favourite of Queen Elizabeth I—it was even rumoured that they were lovers—who led a disastrous expedition against the Irish. His enemies were gathering against him. He made the mistake of relying on the old and doting queen's affection for him. As soon as he reached London he burst into her presence, still in his travelling clothes, unannounced. It is possible that the queen could not cope with this unsubjectlike behaviour; or that she had tired of his swashbuckling policies. At all events he was soon after executed on a trumped-up charge of treason.

I said that the title, 'Girl by a Window,' was meant to suggest

Vermeer—though the poem is still understandable even if you don't recognise the reference. Baroque painters would often use the device of a painting within a painting as a kind of metaphor for what was really going on. The section about Essex functions in this way.

The girl is by the window, stirred by her own sexuality, perhaps puzzled or dismayed by it. The sunlight plays on her features, insistent yet unobtrusive. It is 'surreptitious and impersonal as a night-watchman's cry'—twelve o' clock and all's well, a comforting cry, a sign of the passage of time being tamed into human control. The earl of Essex had burst in on the queen, frightened her into what the middle ages would have called a display of 'danger'—from the same root as 'dominance.' She had acted as a queen, as a great lord affronted: her 'danger' was as much part of womanhood as her ability to love. The girl is poised to reject sexuality as the queen rejected Essex, but the sun, though he is 'tugged naughtily by wet,' kneels unobtrusively 'in a far corner' of her flesh, wiser than a lover, yet like the night-watchman impersonally reminding her that time is passing and that sex is greater than she knows.

Clearly I could not go on just writing poems as if they were paintings. I prefer to put it like that, rather than poems about paintings, for in the case of 'Girl by a Window' the poem is not about a painting but about a girl—actually a specific girl, in a real biographical situation. It alludes to Vermeer but it is not one of Vermeer's pictures. It is not even a picture one can imagine Vermeer painting.

I could not go on for ever 'writing paintings.' But what I found in Neep's work did not stop with that. Previously I had thought of words, phrases, sentences and so on as musical phrases, controlled by the verbs. Now I was making another kind of dance with them, not the musician's but the painter's.* Phrases and sentences become brush-strokes, gestures with the palette knife or the fingers. Looked at in this way, the nouns and adjectives become as

---

* And sometimes the sculptor's—or at least the modeller's—carving in words is a concept I am not sure I understand.

important as verbs. A poetry dominated by its verbs will be a poetry of process, of action. The doer of the action or the circumstances in which it is done will be less important than what is done; but a poetry where nouns and adjectives are dominant is bound to be much more circumstantial about particular people and things, and therefore harder to control. Relevance becomes problematic, as does the question of private knowledge. For instance, have I succeeded in making a public poem about this particular girl by a window, or will the reader complain that he does not know enough of the background to understand what I am doing? Have I given him or her enough clues? Or (equally likely) have I included too many details that merely distract from the meaning?

If you think of an utterance as a series of brush-strokes, then the individual dab of paint can be as short as you like, down to the minimum of a single word. Chinese poetry is based on the number of words in a line—all Chinese words have only one syllable, so in practice, in Chinese, a five-word line is also a five-syllable one. But to call Chinese poetry syllabic is misleading. Every word or syllable has just about equal weight. One is in fact operating a kind of pointillism. In this imitation I have ignored the monosyllabic nature of Chinese words and written in a five-word metre, irrespective of how long the words are:

JEALOUSY IN WINTER

Grey fish shadow through ice.
Robin. Thin legs. Black twig.
Dark world hides below white.
Horned sailors earth brown rig.

I stir tea, thinking you.
Pride shelters below strange walls.
You speak snow-man talk.
Furred urchins crush bright balls.

White fishes round you splash.
My envy hugs guttering fire.
Bronze shadows tomb my corners.
Hope where even fish expire . . .

Individual words set themselves at angles to each other as you say them. Each word is a separate dab of paint. Syntax is reduced to a bare minimum and is often ambiguous. There seems little distinction between parts of speech. The winter scene—the fish under the ice, the robin on the twig, the sailors pulling their boat onto the strand—is sketched in with thick strokes. The second stanza is more inward. I am making a cup of tea looking through the window where 'you' are playing in the snow with the children. I am too proud to join in. Or perhaps I am not invited. I am like the grey fish sheltering under the ice. My envy hugs a guttering fire. Round you, though, the white fishes—snowballs or children—are splashing. The shadows behind me, bronzed by the fire, are where my jealousy would like to see those fish expire.

What emerges from such a poem is a construct where words are fitted together very precisely but in an ambiguous way. It really does not matter what path you follow through the maze. There may well be other solutions which make as much sense as the one I've just outlined. The expressionist value of such a technique in English is perhaps limited, but real enough. For example, it can express the precisions as well as the short-sightedness of jealousy. It plays with all the ambiguities that pander to a fit of the sulks.

'Galilee' is a good deal more serious, but at the same time more problematic. I think it is probably better to let it appear first in its original (1962) version, in order to see what the problems are.

GALILEE

for Els, on her happiness

You were suddenly filling the room like light,
Bewildering the dust of many hard instants
Into diamonds, into bright configurations.

You were everywhere laughing and dancing,
To beg pardon of the room, being so lately
Come into exuberance, clumsily, like light
Of the drawn morning into sleepy eyes.

And only the last time, two months ago, I'd called
Like a conspirator, and crossed you on the stairs
With only bare respect to nail us where we stood.

The iron minutes had creaked to their dully
Embarrassed strike, in the indifferent dread
Of a judge telling time, giving sentence.

Was I warder, you prisoner? Iron minutes
Could not have told the victim from the plot's
Deracination of the free heart, barbarous
As jackboots into every yard of Europe.

And now you were filling the room, suddenly, like light
Over hoarse rigging, knuckles raw through a black night's
Long tussle with the wind, in a hunched smack at sea.

I heard my own voice (among many) trouble the god
Who slept in our stark need, washed by the fathoms
As an entering bone in inventories of coral.

And I heard his woken reproach, suddenly, like light,
Tune down the black winds, and the wavelets
Half-clumsily trip to the harp's plucked reel.

My own heart—O heart of small faith—glittered
In the room like the hard dust of minutes
Suddenly, in the warm joy, bewildered into stars.

Musically, the poem is in three-part or ternary form, A-B-A, though the main image of the A-material—in fact the main idea of the poem—does not occur till the second time round. Section A (stanzas 1-2 and 6-9) is in the imperfect and past definite, while Section B (stanzas 3-5) is mainly in the pluperfect. B had taken place two months before A, and offers a quite different range of imagery: conspirators, courts of law, crucifixion, the Second World War in Europe, as against light, curtains being drawn in the morning, diamonds and stars, and then, second time round, the disciples fishing all night in a storm on the Sea of Galilee and appealing to Christ to save them.

Those are the main images, and already they present a very complicated pattern for so short a poem. It is worth while to look at it in painterly terms, however, not just as music. The brushstrokes of 'Into diamonds, into bright configurations' or 'like light / Of the drawn morning into sleepy eyes,' are quite different from my earlier choreographic style, as in 'One Morning' from *Metamorphoses*. Or again, 'the wavelets half-clumsily tripping to the harp's plucked reel,' though it sounds a musical image, is in fact well within the suggestive range of impressionistic painting. Given that the large-scale structures are musical, the local effects are almost all of a kind that I had learnt from Victor Neep.

I remember at that time I actually tried to paint a picture with oils. My physical handicap has never allowed me to be proficient with any kind of paints, though I have always enjoyed drawing. Even so, oils gave me a shock—I'd only been used to watercolour until then. They were so fluid, so riotously wilful. One thing just led to another. Their physicality amazed me. Using them was far more like modelling with clay than drawing or painting with watercolours.

The way in this poem images sprout images, with the mind hardly in control, seems to me a bit like that:

> And now you were filling the room, suddenly, like light
> Over hoarse rigging, knuckles raw through a black night's
> Long tussle with the wind, in a hunched smack at sea.
>
> I heard my own voice (among many) trouble the god
> Who slept in our stark need, washed by the fathoms
> As an entering bone in inventories of coral.
>
> And I heard his woken reproach, suddenly, like light,
> Tune down the black winds, and the wavelets
> Half-clumsily trip to the harp's plucked reel.

The girl's entry is being compared to light coming after a long stormy night in a boat; and to Christ ('the god') woken by our anxious supplications and calming the winds. Christ's sleep is then compared to a bone underwater, washed by the fathoms; and the bone is finally described as an entry in an inventory of coral.

There are thus four layers of metaphor—light, Christ, bone, inventory—one on top of another. And in the stanza after that, Christ's reproach is like light, it 'tunes down' the winds as though they were a radio set, so that the wavelets begin to dance to a reel played on a harp. Here again, there are four or five different layers—Christ, light, radio set, reel on a harp some of which overlap with the first four. There is also a pun between two of the layers—'tuning' and 'harp's plucked reel.'

Neep's paintings were built up layer by layer, letting each dry for a day or two before adding a new one. Each painting had its own archaeology, and you could see some of the bumps and brush-strokes of earlier layers showing on the surface, as well as the very special kind of luminosity that this process gives you. Was I trying to imitate that multi-level effect in words? Or was I simply giving to words the sort of plasticity and wilfulness I had found in oils? There is no doubt in my mind, however, that the piling of metaphors, one on top of another, was both deliberate and derived from a painterly source.

The plushness and baroque twiddles of the style were altogether too much of a good thing. The great need now was to simplify the textures and keep the mind on the object. At the same time, 'Galilee' was a serious poem, a 'muckle sang,' as the Scots might say, in the main line of my development: for the central concern of my poetry up till 1967 was the achievement of a language in which personal and inter-personal matters could be expressed in ways which were not empiricist and owed nothing to the circumstantial techniques of the novel. 'Galilee' was clearly an important step in that direction. Both in its plethora of images and in its handling, it took risks that were worth taking—the 'jackboots into every yard of Europe' for instance, or using Christ as a bit of pagan mythology, 'the god,' and then coming back into a traditional Christian tone at the end—'O heart of small faith.'

Normally in the process of revision one can cut out all the complications that are not vital to the poem, clean the excrescences away, make the texture more transparent and clarify the thought. It is perfectly possible to do this with 'Galilee.'

The only difficulty is to know where to stop:

GALILEE

You were suddenly filling the room like light,
bewildering the dust of many hard instants
into diamonds, into bright configurations.

Only the last time I'd called
like a conspirator. Iron minutes
creaked to their embarassed strike
like a judge telling time, giving sentence.

Now you were filling the room, like light
over hoarse rigging, knuckled raw
through a long night's tussle with the wind
in a hunched smack at sea.

I heard my own voice trouble the god
who slept in our stark need,

and I heard his woken reproach, like light,
tune down the black winds.

My own heart of small faith glittered
in the room like the hard dust of minutes
suddenly, in warm joy, bewildered into stars.

    I am conscious of loss in this version: 'everywhere laughing and dancing, to beg pardon of the room' from stanza 2 is a good thing to have said; 'in warm joy' in the last line is thinner than 'in the warm joy' of the original; and I miss the exclamation, old-fashioned though it sounds—'O heart of small faith.' And so on. To revise a poem against its grain like this means you have to re-write the whole thing in a consistent way; and that inevitably risks throwing the baby out with the bath water. So far I have not found a middle way, and therefore, as the original will not do, the above revision has to stand. But I cannot say that the position is satisfactory. In neither version, incidentally, am I sure that the reader is given enough clues in the B-section as to what happened two months ago.
    The great need after 'Galilee' was to simplify the textures and

keep your eye on the object. The trouble is if you do that and keep to a painterly approach, what you end up with is something very close to imagism. These two short poems about snow followed 'Galilee' a couple of months later:

> SNOW (1)
>
> A tree,
> a black explosion of stillness,
> lifting through nights
> the dry white fire
> of a myriad creaking fingers.
>
> SNOW (2)
>
> What was once
> slim girlhood
> under the moon
>
> starves
>
> and bitterly forgets
> mufflered children
> holing
> the crisp light
>
> with squeezed-in
> fingerfuls
> out of the
> bouncing
> ground.

Imagism is almost where modern poetry began. I had no wish to begin it all over again, and in any case I don't think I would ever have been good at it. For me, imagism has always been a place to visit for a holiday, or to prove some kind of point. I don't think

I've ever been tempted to live there permanently. You have to be an English empiricist to do that.

*   *   *

Nevertheless the painter's hand has taught me a great deal over the years. I have been influenced by other painters since then— Clive Walley, Alan McPherson, Michael Cullimore, Paul Davies— but perhaps never in so painterly a way. Victor Neep died in Caernarfon in January 1979. His son Paul suggested that I should write an epitaph to put on his grave, so I wrote this *englyn milwr* (soldier's *englyn*, a three-line poem with rhyme and *cynghanedd*) coming home from his funeral:

DAYTIME MOON

Even under the glare of noonday
this thin mother-of-pearl inlay
on the heart, stands in the way.

CONTEMPLATIVE POETRY

Catholic theologians distinguish two kinds of prayer. The first kind depends on marshalling the mind and will consciously to attend on God and his revelation in and through Jesus the Christ. The imagination is encouraged to present lively images, from the Scriptures and elsewhere, that illustrate God's mercy to us and his love. The praying self identifies with the characters in the Gospel who respond to Jesus. We look at ourselves in the light of the Prodigal Son, or the woman taken in adultery, or Peter denying his master three times before cockcrow; and we pray verbally with them that our sins may be forgiven and our faith made strong in the community of the faithful. Or perhaps we do not use words, but let our minds and imaginations be caught up in the wonder and folly of God; for that is the highest kind of praise, where Satan fell. This kind of prayer the theologians call 'meditation.'

But there are some people (possibly a great many, if the truth were told) who, either always or at a certain time in their lives, do not seem able to follow through this way of prayer. They start to meditate, and yes, the images, the thoughts, the feelings flow from them, they feel exalted; but then trapped in an endless regress of mirrors, or distracted from God rather than drawn towards him. Suddenly there is bewilderment and a sense that this 'meditation' is not what they ought to be doing.

They may be called, say the theologians, to the other life of prayer, that of 'contemplation'—or they may be just glimpsing, just visiting the sepulchre -

> O my soul, look! Chief of kings, author
> Of peace, he lay in that room,
> The creation in him moving
> And he a dead man in the tomb!

Traditionally the contemplative life finds its symbol, not in the empty tomb of the Resurrection but in the dead Christ lying hidden in it on Holy Saturday—'Song and life of the lost,' as Ann Griffiths calls it. This song is Christ's yoga, the final emptying of the son of Man, the passing away of desire in his Buddhahood, the enlightenment of the True Light, the final darkness, the authority of peace.

Contemplation is to make yourself that tomb. As a sepulchre you do not know who is laid in you. You must live that ignorance to the full. You have only the blind eyes of bare faith to look who it is. Blindness is the pattern you must fit yourself to. Tap tap around the room with your blindman's stick. No, that too is a distraction. You are sepulchre, nothing else. You are not even that particular sepulchre in that particular garden where particular arms laid him like a guest in you, those two thousand years ago. Because that sepulchre can be imagined, it is not where you are or what you should be doing.

Or at least, not looking at the images, not letting yourself follow them. Yet there is a darkness in the imagining itself. By putting yourself wholly into the imagining, and not into what is imagined—as into tasting food, rather than the food itself—a kind of contemplation is possible. In the actual moment of the generation of images there is a secret door into what is imageless, as there is in the now of everything we do. But it is a hard door to keep open—easy enough to glimpse but difficult to work at because the images are so close and they can so easily be merely distracting. There are contemplatives who use this door however, and in India and the east there are ways made of it.

It is confusing that in the eastern religions the devotees call 'meditation' what Christians call 'contemplation'.

You go into darkness, to be sepulchre, to be unknowing. You go in the name of love, in the name of joy, but it is widowhood you go to. The mind tears at you in panic, the imagination flares with its picture writing of dreams. You must calm your will to ignore them. It is the folly of God, that you, the sparrow of time, must fall. It is his business to grieve for the fall of that sparrow, not yours. You are sepulchre. It is his business if he chooses to die like the sparrow. You wait like the darkness where they may have laid the tiny body of God. No, yet again, the images creep back. You are not like anything, not like darkness or like a tomb. Jesus the Christ is no wren king, no tattered fragment of feathers killed in the hedges on Stephen's Day. You are sepulchre. You are nothing.

Speak if you must, whisper the meaningless rigmaroles of prayer. They give the mind something to do. But you must not try to follow the words into meaning because their lack of meaning for you is why you are here.

*   *   *

When I was describing what happened when I wrote a poem during the year or two when I had a Muse called Liz, my story was this:

> For perhaps a day or two before a poem, I wandered around feeling haunted and irritable. Then, usually last thing at night, when I was dog-tired, sometimes so tired I was choking with it, it cornered me. I would often kneel with my head in an armchair, going down, down, down. Sometimes I would make desultory prayers—more to give my consciousness something to do, like Alice looking at the various shelves on her way down the rabbit hole, than for any religious reason. The darkness itself was the religious thing . . .
>
> Suddenly I was sitting in front of a typewriter with a clean sheet of paper in it, typing. Words would wash over me, all kinds of words, beautiful, ugly words, They were irrelevant, but some of them I usually managed to write down. Then a phrase, or a line or two, would come that had power. Liz was all round me, I was talking to her. The poem was there. After that, it was more like delivering a baby than anything else. Pulling it out whole. Sometimes, for a minute or two, the tension would break and I would surface, light a cigarette or walk round the room. Then back again, into the darkness.

Just as the more 'normal' processes of writing poetry, emotion recollected in tranquility for instance, have a great similarity to what the theologians call meditation, so it is obvious that contemplative prayer and the way I wrote poetry to Liz* have much in common. They both begin with frustration. They both involve going down into an imageless darkness, using verbal prayer in a 'meaningless' way. Both processes tend to engender a flood of irrelevant words and images as the imagination's normal functioning is superseded. A certain violence in the poetic process may be discounted. Contemplative monks make a habit of contemplation: they do it every day in controlled situations, whereas a poet's inspiration is not a habitual state and has therefore more resistance to overcome each time it happens. But even with monks, violence is common enough. Japanese Buddhism, for instance, is full of Zen masters knocking their disciples down, or vice versa, in the give and take of Enlightenment. There is nothing effete or otherworldly about the practice of contemplation.

The two obvious differences between contemplative prayer and the inspiration I have described is that inspiration finds someone there (the presence of the Muse all round you) and that it results in the creation of a poem. Let me take these differences separately.

The poem first. This is what the poet goes down into the darkness to find. His purpose is quasi-shamanistic, a kind of exercise in shape-shifting, a journey to another world. In that sense his going into the darkness is applied contemplation, lacking perhaps the purity of contemplative prayer. On the other hand, to write a poem is not strictly an ulterior motive. He simply goes into the darkness and does what he has to do. If the poem is not there to be written (and sometimes it is not) his journey is not wasted.

---

* I would like to disclaim any attempt to legislate for poets. Good poems can be written in many different ways, some of which it would be very hard to call 'inspiration' at all. My 'story' is in fact just a story: an account which to the best of my recollection matches the way many of my poems at that time were written. I think that the process is sufficiently interesting and important to justify telling this 'story,' despite the vagueness and subjectivity which necessarily attends it.

Much of his life's meaning and reality is hidden from his normal self. He is moving about 'in worlds not realised,' and his poems are clues brought back from a hidden country. He may not fully understand what they are saying, not for many years afterwards.

The presence of the Muse is more an apparent difficulty than a real one. I have shown in my essay on the Muse that though muses are very varied in their effects on those they inspire, almost always they function as guides. They lead the imagination into new territory. There is often a point in the relationship when their job is done and they leave the poet to his own devices. When Liz left Bangor and I could no longer hope for her inspiration, I did not stop going down into the darkness for poems. Other girls, to some extent, served as surrogate muses, but they were most of them hardly more than a trigger, and some important poems at that time were written without any muse at all. A lot of them, in fact, are attempts to come to terms with a darkness that has not even the comfort of a Muse to console me.

Looked at in this way, 'The Marsh' seems to express a state not unlike what St John of the Cross calls 'the dark night of the senses,' when the soul has turned to the darkness to seek for God, so that the sensual world is dead or a mere temptation to you. You have lost the world but you have not yet found God. All that is left is the ravenous, desperate selfhood.

THE MARSH

At the numb root
I know winter,
I am marsh.

Tattering reeds
dip broken into ice-logged weeds.

The beggaring wind
is an anguish
day and night,
work and desperation and play.

There is nowhere opposed to the wind
any vertical bastion,
any barn or tree
that is defiant.

All of me
is distance.

To the four horizons
tiredness
devours the land.

I become
tired silt
at the root.

*

Since the caking fen
where the cheeks
of the crawling lungfish
heaved and plopped —

So erudite of water, now to probe
in this half-land
for their worms —

Since the unbent light disturbed
their vague
fishy eyes —

Dry land prefigured me
who now to distance
am bespattered out,

torn
by the bare identity
I AM

> into black silt
> under the wind.

I compare my state of being to that of the first land animal, a primitive lungfish forced by drought to leave the water and earn a precarious living in the drying mud. (Underwater light is refracted or bent at the surface: this is the first time the fish's eyes have looked with unbent light). I am bespattered over the landscape as if by an explosion, torn 'by the bare identity I AM.' What is this bare identity? Is it the ego, whose nakedness is now revealed as self-destructive? But 'I AM' or its double form, 'I AM WHO AM' is the name of God. When Christ said, 'Before Abraham and Isaac, I am,' he is traditionally understood to be naming himself as the Deity.

So there is already in this sequence one of the main problems of the Way of Contemplation. Mystics (that is, advanced contemplatives) are often accused of talking about God when they mean themselves, and of talking about themselves in a way that is only proper about Deity. In India the holy man surrounded by his disciples is in some sense God. He is referred to in Western literature as a God-man. Indian theology is more tolerant than ours, because it places the Unity of things at the centre of the diversity. Indians tend to say that we approach Reality—Godhead—as we journey to the one centre, that is, to the true self. In the West, as in Islam, this kind of talk is generally felt as blasphemous, a sin which occupies a surprisingly central place in our civilization. It was Christ's 'blasphemy' which delivered him to be crucified.

The bare identity of God or the bare identity of the self (as distinguished from the ego) tears me like an explosion,

> into black silt
> under the wind.

In the next poem of this group, I call out to the Muse—not Liz, she had left by then—as the Egyptian goddess Isis. When the god Osiris was killed, his body was scattered in a million pieces over the whole land. Isis went in search of him, gathering the fragments of his flesh until she had the complete body of the god whom she then nursed back into life.

ISIS

From the silver field of my death
a shy angel
upright and green
centres the hollow disc of my disquiet
like a child saboteur.

Isis of compassion—radius—
road of my healing—

Gather the speckled courage from my silt.
Make cosmos pivot on deed.
Flicker tall shadows.
Be man.

The shy angel rising in the midst of a featureless landscape the silver field—suddenly gives a focus to 'the hollow disc of my disquiet'; its presence is alarming, against nature in such a place, 'like a child saboteur'. Though the angel is recognised as Isis the mother goddess, this disquiet is not totally resolved. I ask for her help, in this marsh. As if I were Osiris I plead with her to gather me together, recreate the ego that had been scattered as silt, make me a man again. But isn't this really to sabotage why I am scattered like this in the first place?

* * *

These poems are not necessarily testimonies of personal experience. They are imaginative constructs, like all my poems. They do not represent experience so much as create it. The relationship between 'what happens' to the poet in real life (supposing that concept makes sense) and his imaginative creation in the poem is a complex one, and presumably varies from poet to poet and even from poem to poem. So if I say that 'The Marsh' expresses a state of being similar to St John of the Cross's 'dark night of the senses' I am not saying that when I wrote it I was in that dark night. I may have been, but I had no spiritual adviser to tell me. The individual cast loose in the world is not to be trusted to diagnose these things.

In any case during this time, or soon after, I was probably busier than I have ever been before or since. I started seriously on the job of translating Welsh poetry for *The Penguin Book of Welsh Verse*. Translation shares with inspiration a lot of frustration: over short distances I found myself going in and out of a darkness similar to the one where I wrote poems. It was, as it were, inspiration simmering, not on the boil.

Many of the poems of this period describe waiting or states of being between events—'Girl by a Window,' for instance, or love poems like 'Moss':

MOSS

Black moss under moss moon.
This night two ponder rock.
Frogs comma the moist dark.
Obstinate streams sing like shock.

Though we sit separate nights
thirsts have their margin soon.
Oasis, I pull you down,
gazelle, to drink moss moon.

The desert of thirst is a metaphor for the lovers' separation. I represent myself as the oasis where my lover, the gazelle, is soon going to drink, at a mossy pool where the moon surrounded by cirrus clouds ('moss moon') is reflected. In many of these love poems (but not all) the sexual love is suffused by that of the spirit, as it is in much Persian poetry and in the traditional 'mystical' interpretation of the biblical love-songs in the *Song of Songs*. This little poem, for instance, could be interpreted as God the lover's offering himself as water to the soul, the gazelle, and telling her that her thirsting will soon be over. This is rather an extreme case, and even here such an allegorical reading seems forced: I think more commonly the love poetry is simply expressive of a state of being analogous to that of the soul's waiting upon God.

Another kind of poem is that of the Holy Fool and his analogues. It is typical of the contemplative mind to delight in paradox and even in pure nonsense. R.S. Thomas, for instance, in his later poems often seems to be playing games with God, and God with him. Here is an example of the Holy Fool archetype in my own work:

ANYTHING

> Maybe hidden in the simplicity
> of its own anywhere-
> reaching radiance,
>
> Anyhow
> he could not look through to see it.
> He wambles round everywhere,
>
> generates everytime in his
> grotesque
> suburb of wishes,
>
> ripples perhaps
> from the unique centre,
>
> Anytime
> maybe hidden in the complexity
> wambling round it in an untidy ring
>
> where the red admiral settles on the thyme,
> where the boy in the park throws at the čonker tree
> sticks, bones, pebbles, to wit: anything.

The poem was originally a sonnet: the last six lines still preserve the rhyme-scheme of the sestet. A girl came up to me in a party. 'Write me a poem,' she said. 'What kind of a poem?' I said. 'A sonnet,' she said. 'What about?' I said. 'Oh, anything,' she said. So I did.

The indefinite pronouns and adverbs—anything, everything,

and so on—have a fascinatingly slippy kind of syntax. We all remember Odysseus tricking Polyphemus by saying that his name was 'Nobody.' The other Cyclops heard him yelling in agony because Odysseus had put out his only eye, but when they asked him who had done it, all he could say was 'Nobody did it' so Odysseus escaped.

The Holy Fool is searching for—what? For anything. For the unpredictable arbitrary datum, for the open secret of what is now, for the only real knowledge we have. In chemistry, the element hydrogen in its normal molecular form is a relatively inert gas. But when it has just been formed by a chemical reaction, before it has had time to combine two by two into molecules, it has very different properties, behaving as a strong reagent, almost like chlorine. It is called 'nascent' or atomic hydrogen. If we could only recover the *nascency* of things—of anything—we should be looking at the world as it comes from the hands of God.

'Anything' is maybe hidden in its own radiance. The fool can't see it for looking, his desires are continually making 'everytime' and 'everywhere' instead of the unique moment. The complexity of everything hides the real simplicity of anything. The paraphrase is banal enough, but the point of the poem is the way it acts out its meaning, so that 'sticks, bones, pebbles' emerge out of the punning syntax as physical objects with their nascency still potent. They are still 'anything,' or at any rate the nearest that words can go towards it: for of course to talk or even to think about anything is to hide from its thingness.

I suppose that of all the great writers of our century, Samuel Beckett is the contemplative *par excellence*. T.S. Eliot talks a lot about the contemplative tradition, but so much of it remains talk; and R.S. Thomas, though he is certainly writing out of contemplative experience, is tentative and unsupported by his *milieu*. Beckett's strange, atheistic darkness is very pure. All his plays are fantasies on the theme of contemplation, wild parodies on the tradition which would do credit to a Zen master. *Waiting for Godot* in its very name sums it up. The plays get closer and closer to silence, the aural darkness of an empty stage.

I mention Beckett because certain of my poems from the middle sixties might remind you of his creatures. By the side of his mastery, my vision in this field seems small. However, I did not at that time know his work. Here is a poem about the holy fool of contemplation as a kind of Easter Island statue shat upon by the gods:

A KING SEATED IN THE SUMPS OF TIME

> Silt's grey foliage
> where I am throned
> proliferates.
> The gods roost all around me.
> Loudly
> like rookeries
> their beaks scream.
>
> They foul me with their droppings.
> My eyes
> are oracular pits
> of the devastation of cities.
>
> My mouth
> is smaller
> than the articulation
> of prayer.
>
> One day
> I shall
> utter it.

* * *

I would go to quite extreme lengths to have a poem come upon me unawares, so that its nascent force would take me with it. By 'unawares' I don't necessarily mean that I took no notice of a poem that was coming: but that its subject, style and form had to be shaped in the moments of inspiration, not beforehand. Let me give an example.

My friend Bernard Rands the composer was very excited by the unexplored possibilities of the harp. At one stage he was planning a book on the subject, and he asked me to write a poem to be a frontispiece.

Two problems faced me. First, how to make a poem that would look like a frontispiece. To put the title at the top, I thought, would give it too much the air of a separate work. So the title had to go in the middle. When the poem was read aloud, it had to be broken in two by the sort of pause and tone of voice that announces a new title; and after a similar pause, had to continue as if nothing had happened.

Second, the idea of a harp is sunk deep in poetic commonplace. At all costs I had to escape from the traditional associations—bards, angels, King David and so on. I decided to appeal directly to my subconscious, and write down a list of words by free association with HARP. These I would then use as the framework of my poem. Here is the list I wrote down:

>DUSK
>HEADLIGHT
>JAB
>WOUND
>STAR
>FELICITY
>WRONG
>TOOTHACHE
>LIMPOPO
>MORSE
>ELEPHANTS
>GANGRENE
>TOMTOMS
>STAR
>REPUBLIC
>REASONS OF THE WATER
>HOLOCAUST
>DROP OF DEW

The Elephant Child in Kipling's *Just-So Stories*, growing his trunk by the great grey green greasy Limpopo River, was obviously at the back of my mind; but here is the poem I wrote:

The felicity of the Republic like a toothache
jabs headlight on headlight
into the Limpopo night.

Elephants
peruse the reasons of the water.
The felicity of the Republic gaps the dusk
with many a plosive tusk.

Tangles of the tomtom crouch
in the sharp

FANTASIA FOR THE HARP

felicity that might be worse
(it might be morse)

Can no one rid me of this vexing wave —
is no one brave enough to brake
the solemn Limpopo?

Holocausts
of silence run arterially
in the sudden stroke of a star.

The felicity of the Kingdom, cold and true,
gathers the Limpopo water
into a single drop of dew.

 Alas, Bernard's book on the harp in modern music never materialised. Whether, if it had, he would have used my poem, I don't know. Its connection with the instrument is perhaps more a question of sound than sense. I can hear the harp in it—all those p's and k's, and the whole whirl of imagery ending on 'drop of dew.' But I think I was too exuberant, too sardonic and playful— like the Crocodile to the Elephant Child. Anyhow, it is no good having a frontispiece without a book. Accordingly I have revised the poem, cutting out the harp and trying to clarify the meaning for the general reader.

What the poem is actually about is the traffic on a busy road at night. The headlights of the approaching cars spread out like tusks of elephants filing down to drink in the Limpopo; at another level they are like the shooting pains of toothache, one after the other. Henry II asked about Thomas à Becket, 'Will no one rid me of this troublesome priest?' The cars are the felicity of the Republic—the world's happiness; but there is another kind of felicity, that of the Kingdom sought in silence and contemplation, in which the bustle of the whole world—the Limpopo water—is gathered into a single dewdrop.

MEDITATION ON A NIGHT-TIME MOTORWAY

The felicity of the Republic like a toothache
jabs headlight on headlight
into the Limpopo night.

Elephants
peruse the reasons of the water.
the felicity of the Republic gaps the dusk
with many a plosive tusk.

Can no one rid me of this vexing wave —
is no one brave enough to brake
the solemn Limpopo?

Holocausts
of silence run arterially
in the sudden stroke of a star.

The felicity of the Kingdom, cold and true,
gathers the Limpopo water
into a single drop of dew.

Lastly, here is a poem called 'Shell.' It is the first poem I have so far considered in these essays that looks initially as if it might be a typical modern English poem. It presents an imaginative picture of a sea-snail living and dead on the beach. It is even 'creative writing,' the decoration of a single image or theme with daring *mots justes* kept in control with a slightly ironic tone of voice.

Ah well, the devil can quote Scripture when it suits him. Here is the poem:

SHELL

A snail that would tuck itself,
grouch and gormandise
on the rotted flavours of brown weed
and snuffle down on slime

(its physiognomy precise
with two soft prongs)
has built in the dry dust
its Pyramid, or Ziggurat.

Wedged with cuneiform
a library of stone
where treasure-seekers
like rife semen, curled in

losing themselves along the pearl
into upper rooms—
the God of the Snail empty
among the cobwebs.

And outside,
mongrel echoes on the grey face
are baffled by eroded ciphers
back into sandswept peace.

I will merely point out that it is not the snail-shell that is described as empty, but the God of the Snail. In fact the shell is yet another analogue for the holy sepulchre, the dark tomb where Christ lies empty of the world, like Buddha in Nirvana. ('Baffled,' by the way, does not only mean 'foiled' or 'reduced to perplexity.' A 'baffle' is a board or screen placed to reduce noise or radio interference.)

The snail is like the holy fool. He lives in slime, grouching and gormandising on the rotted flavours of the world; but he also builds in the dry dust his Pyramid or Ziggurat, his shell. Pyramids and Ziggurats were imitation mountains built as temples or tombs for the god-kings in Egypt and Mesopotamia respectively. They were ransacked by thieves looking for the treasure they contain. Cuneiform was the wedge-writing of the ancient Mesopotamians, usually impressed into clay and then baked as tiles.

The snail, like the holy fool of contemplation, has made himself a tomb for God. But the fool is also like the treasure-seeker curling in among the 'upper rooms' and finding the God empty among the cobwebs.

THE WELSHNESS OF THINGS

My poetry began in a proto-modernist way, exploring dream imagery and reflecting the situations I had read about in books—the *Aeneid*, Catullus, Shakespeare, *Paradise Lost* and Verlaine; above all it was preoccupied with form—allegory, sonata form, variations, composition in a painterly sense; what happens when you let a word go for a walk, what happens when you use words or phrases as dabs of paint or as musical motifs. Grammar, particularly syntax. The role of the subconscious, and how to gear it into poetic composition. Various metres, and various un-metres, like biblical parallelism, and why these no longer fitted with the genius of twentieth century English. In fact, I had a thoroughly unrepresentational, unempiricist view of poetry, not essentially very different from that of Dylan Thomas or Vernon Watkins. The last thing I expected poetry to do was to record 'sensible' experience, using the term in a sort of Jane Austen meaning, both 'derived from sense-experience' and 'justifiable to common sense.' In Jungian terms I was not a sensation-type: I lived as an extrovert through intellect and as an introvert through intuition. Insofar as I was philosophically worried—and I was—it was not epistemology that worried me, but ontology. At college I was drawn to rationalists like Plato, Spinoza or Leibniz, and could barely comprehend what Locke and Hume were trying to do.

Welsh poetry impinged on me first as a way out of empiricism—not that I would have put it like that, but English empiricism (and all the other things about English culture that I hated, the class-structure, the 'there there' attitude of superior sympathy) was intensely claustrophobic to me. Something must be allowed for my position as a handicapped person, no doubt, as with Garlick; but it was mainly that empiricism had never taken root in my schooling in Colwyn Bay. My teachers were part English, part Welsh, but the secret of it was Welsh—where the action was, in the next field but one. I only came into contact with real English teaching in my last year in the sixth when a woman started teaching us practical criticism of modern poets like Louis

MacNeice. Once you teach practical criticism or creative writing—the other side of the same coin—you're into empiricism where writing is about experience.

Fortunately or unfortunately, this was soon overlaid by the first two years at Bangor where we studied things like Virgil's *Aeneid*, *The Faery Queene*, symbolic logic and Plato's *Republic*. All of which I loved. We had a lecturer on Spenser who spent weeks detailing exactly what Spenser used the final alexandrine of his stanza for. His were the only English lectures where I bothered to take more than nominal notes, and I still have them. There was a time when English poetry was not wasting our time recording mere experience! And in philosophy, our professor was H.D. Lewis, the intuitionist and philosopher of religion. His Plato course was one of the most deeply satisfying I ever took. Again, you see, Lewis was a halfway house from Welsh rationalism towards empiricism. But no real empiricist could ever tolerate an intuitionist theory, for example, of ethics. You go through all the motions of empiricist analysis to the point of despair, where you deny any empirical basis to morality at all. Then you say, but we are moral creatures. Right and wrong, good and bad, are meaningful concepts. Therefore they must be intuited, not derived from sensation. For an empiricist, of course, it smacks too much of innate ideas, which is where the empiricist critique of rationalism starts—though in fact it probably is not about an innate idea: you are just confronted with moral truth as a kind of 'thou.' You just *know*.

In my second year we did Descartes (whom I thought trivial but quite enjoyable), Spinoza and Liebniz whom I loved and still revere as opening up huge imaginative portals of thought. We did some Kant, but not much. Whereas our discussion of Spinoza and Liebniz was concentrated more on exposition, with Descartes, the empiricists and modern logical positivists we tended to pick holes in their arguments the whole time. Looking back it seems very like a thoroughly Welsh rearguard action.

I became a Christian in my first year, and a Catholic in the two years I was away from Bangor after my M.A. Here again I was being moved in the direction of another kind of rationalism, Aquinas and Aristotle. I read a bit later Maritain's books on aesthetics and Catholicism—things like *Art and Scholasticism*.

Meanwhile my awareness of Welsh praise poetry was growing, as a made thing, where you arbitrarily choose your material rather than it being presented to you by experience—cf. R.S. Thomas's 'Poetry for Supper,' which exactly hits on this major fault-line between English and Welsh traditions. I did a bit of writing in the middle fifties which tried to come close to this ideal—poems for marriages, and an ode for the death of Williams Parry.

But I was too young to grasp all the difficulties, social and cultural, of following a Welsh praise-poetics in English. In any case, I was learning about feeling as a rational faculty of judgement. Most of my work up to 1958 was concerned with feeling as a problem area: that is, something I had to learn about. I wrote a whole series of Horatian odes where my feelings of exile in England were expressed in the small change of the suburban countryside in winter. I don't think most of them work very well— one man said they were too coy—but I was trying to deal with small feelings first, before coping with big ones like patriotism or falling in love or religious excitement. In a way they were attempts at empiricism, but refracted through the rationalism of the classical ode. I also began writing short narrative poems about old men, childhood, pets, relatives, lovers separated by war and so on. Not much is any good but I was learning how you have to use fiction in the feeling-mode. This early phase culminated in a series of love-sonnets 'To Vanna.' The name is short for Giovanna and gestures towards another attempt to know about experience from a rationalist background—in this case, the Italian Dolce Stil Nuovo. I had just translated about eighteen poems from Dante's *Canzoniere* and *La Vita Nuova*, because I had been hopelessly in love with the girlfriend of my best friend and Dante was clearly the expert on that sort of situation. But the Vanna poems were not to her: they are much rawer than most of the Dolce Stil, and Catullan rather than Dantesque in inspiration. The problem was, any attempt to express my emotional experience directly was immediately perceived as arising out of my situation as a spastic, which of course was intensely limiting.

This stalemate was nonetheless pushing me towards an unmodernist poetic, based on representation—where I was competing on alien terms with post-war English poetry as a whole. My whole upbringing and personality, and my provincial status as far as English poetry was concerned, made success in that direction very problematic. Yet it was the poems of this period, collected in a rough and tumble way in *Formal Poems*, *The Margaret Book* and Vol. I of my *Poems 1951-67*, that people apparently liked enough to give me prizes for.

The most deeply rooted faculties of my mind were an extrovert and intensely inquisitive intelligence and an introvert intuition. The dark world of intuition, verging on mysticism, was from the beginning where I felt my home was. In 1951 I wrote a poem 'Three Swans' about the Muse as being beyond world power, religion and death. The trouble was, this claim was purely formal—an empty formula without any relation to the rest of my life. As a presence it loomed over me, sometimes in a terrifying way, sometimes as a comfort, a kind of abstract Celtic twilight where the cry of owl and curlew haunted my senses with intimations of the goddess calling to me through the darkness. I wrote a lot of very bad verse, very self-indulgent, romantic stuff, trying to express this inchoate sense of female mystery, female tragedy as well. For the Muse was always a tragic figure, a *pietà* mourning the loss of her lover and son.

Then in 1954 I wrote a series of mythological sonnets, again not very good, but focussing on one of the main subjects of my poetry in subsequent years—the need to be properly born. Since my disablement as a spastic was, I am told, due to my being born too quickly so that my brain was damaged through lack of oxygen at the crucial moment, it would be very easy to see this theme as a wish-fulfilling fantasy beating forever against the reality of a marred life. Even in terms of my own psychology, however, this is too crude a description. My life was indeed marred, but as much by ill-directed love on the part of those who brought me up as by the physical wounds of birth. I had been given a child's ego, not a man's. I was only half-born, therefore. That is why the theme of birth was not a wish-fulfilment but an imperative. I had to be properly born, to take responsibility for myself as everyone must who is not to be coddled and protected all their life. And of course as an imperative it had wider implications than just me: a properly born ego is a basic human requirement, whether of individuals or societies. That is why I dedicated my poem 'Birth' to Emyr Llywelyn when he was in prison for sabotage directed against the drowning of a Welsh valley, and why I published it in *The Welsh Nation*.

But until 1959 I had not found myself as a poet. In the early spring of that year I 'fell in love' with a muse called Liz, and for the next eight years or so I made poems in her darkness or in the darkness that I first discovered through her. Of all my work, these, collected mostly in Vols. II and III of *Poems 1951-67*, seem to me nearest the centre of my work. They have almost never been noticed by critics, and as a result are largely unknown among poetry-readers, even in Wales.

Partly the trouble is, they hardly describe the outside world at all, except in passing. They are power objects, talismans of process, songs of innocence. I think of them as modernist, with something of the *innocence* of analytical cubism, though in no sense are most of them cubist. They are in the first place not at all about Wales nor do they derive from the Welsh tradition, any more than 'Poem in October' or 'Over Sir John's hill'; but they are full of the countryside of north Wales, north Denbighshire and Arfon in particular, almost against my wishes, so that people who read them often respond to them as if they were souvenirs of their stay in Bangor.

At first they were poems of the subjunctive of possibility; then, when that went sour on me, so that fact and wish were forever asymptotic to each other, I changed to the indicative. They were like contemplative prayer, something so near to impotence and folly and death and yet pressing upon a nameless mystery, a deus absconditus. They image the self as a holy fool, a stone statue dug up from the sandhills, shat upon by seabirds.

And then finally the muse left me, we were sundered by impotence, by the crush of a triumphal march. There was a crisis in which I had to recognise my child-like ego for what it was, no fit self for a man. I climbed out of the darkness into the anti-humanism of modernist strip lighting. I was a man in a world of monopoly capitalism, where personal worth was resolved into exchange value, as the Communist Manifesto put it. I discovered my Prospero's Island—yea, all which it inherits—were luxury goods, spices to add wit to the concoctions of frilly-aproned young wives.

In a series of prose-poems, cantatas and concrete called 'Claim, Claim, Claim' (after a piece designed for music set in an insurance office) I explored this high capitalist sensibility, a world where experience is peddled like cocaine, where computers ask each other metaphysical questions, where the past is grown like exotic plants in a glasshouse, where the natural surrealism of cities does not hide the delicacy of old men's tenderness or despair.

And it broke in my hands. I heard the clutter of pop-festivals, of comedians, old women. Sally in our alley was suddenly more important than the Director in his boardroom. No, I didn't want to go back to all the dreary representational poetry of experience. But still, I recalled that of the four mental faculties of Jung, Intellect, Feeling, Sensation and Intuition, two only were thoroughly in place in my poetry, the two I had started with, extrovert intelligence and introvert intuition. One other, feeling, had been bespoken for, as it were, before the muse years. It was time to look at things, to hear them, to run my fingers over surfaces, to taste and smell them. Not because that was part of my experience, but as an act of arbitrary acquisition, something given, a Gift.

For what broke in my hands that year in 1969 was modernism itself. I wanted freedom to move, to invent my own story, to be arbitrary and affectionate—

> Claim of the mortal man in the midmost of his way
> in the light years of heaven a fathom of darkness
>
> Claim of the girlhood and the boyhood of things
> In the breakdown of stars, to be awkward and rich
>
> Claim of the angel to realise the brute,
> Claim of the living to death, of the dying to live

And I asked myself —

> WHAT IS THE EMPTINESS
> WHAT IS THE MIDGET
>
>   query: and the heroes?

AND THE HEROES

WHAT IS STOLEN
WHAT HAVE THE EMPTINESS AND THE STOLEN AND
THE GOLD

                                        query: together?

TOGETHER TO DO WITH
TOGETHER TO CONTRAST WITH
TOGETHER TO IDENTIFY WITH
TOGETHER TO GIVE

                                        what is

QUERY: STRUCTURE?

                                        what is

WHAT IS

                                        what is made
                                        what is free

Out of that question come the Gift Poems. They are made and they are free. I suppose they are post-modernist. They invent their own story. They are quite arbitrary in their subject-matter, the gift itself. It can be a bit of slate, a silver spoon, a fern leaf, a lily seed. As arbitrary in their own way, and as deliberately chosen, as Frank O'Hara walking into a shop in New York and buying a book to give to one of his mates. As arbitrary as Dafydd ap Gwilym sending a seagull to his girlfriend to tell her he loves her and three traditions of poetry don't equal what he sees in her. As arbitrary and as meticulously described: for this *dyfalu* or comparison-finding is where the faculty of sensation is triumphant. Sensation is an irrational business—that is what is so dead about most English imagism, and about Welsh imitations of it like Minhinnick's, it tries to describe objects as if they were there to be part of the author's growing, as if they were organic to him, and therefore amenable to judgement. Listen to Dafydd:

> Your beauty's immaculate,
> Shard like the sun, brine's gauntlet.
> You're buoyant on the deep flood,
> A proud swift bird of fishfood.
> You'd ride at anchor with me,
> Hand in hand there, sea lily.
> Like a letter, a bright earnest,
> You're a nun on the tide's crest.

He is friendly to what he sees, but he doesn't usurp its space. He doesn't try to make it an objective correlative. If it's a letter, yes, he can deliver it, he can tell it what he wants it to say. And then we realise that this seagull is both a bird he has seen paddling in Cricieth bay and a part of a story he is inventing. In both capacities it is made, it is free.

So in writing my Gifts I was indeed conscious of Dafydd ap Gwilym. I developed what I called an epode, from Horace's first book of lyrics, not quite an ode. As in Horace it is in quatrains, with the first and third lines longer than the second and fourth. In my epodes, but not in Horace's, the rhythm is largely free, but on the whole the second and fourth lines have two stresses and rhyme in some way. The idea is not to produce perfect self-contained stanzas but a sort of counterpoint of quatrain, rhyme and sentence structure, so that the relation of quatrains to each other is as fluid and as full of interruptions as the relation of couplets in a Dafydd ap Gwilym *cywydd*. Although it was not remotely like a *cywydd*, with a quite different speed and discursiveness, yet the epode enabled me to do the sort of thing in twentieth century English that the *cywydd* did in fourteenth-century Welsh. It can be arbitrary, digressive, brilliant, self-indulgent, aphoristic; or it can tell stories, give little lectures, praise—all the things that modern English representational poetry as well as classical modernism tells you you ought not to do.

I confess also that I wanted to solve a personal problem. We live in an increasingly gift-giving civilization. Wherever you go gift shoppes sprout over the terrain. Our economy seems to be largely based on the orgy of gift-giving that goes on at Christmas. (You wouldn't realise this salient fact from modern poetry, would you?)

Now gift-giving is something I am very bad at. I was never taught to do it. If I tried to give anything to my relations as a child I was kindly told I should not waste my money. So I get frustrated, tense, neurotic and weary with the effort of the unreason involved and the fact that I cannot see why one gift is better to buy than any other. Why not just get something at random—a stone or a bit of stick—and personalise it with a poem? After all, it's the thought that counts, they say, and I am quite good at thought.

Anyhow it worked. The Gift Poems solved both my problems at once. They gave what is made and what is free, and they delighted their recipients as no presents of mine had ever done before.

And that takes us down to 1971, where we can pause for a moment as a new phase of my life was beginning. *The Penguin Book of Welsh Verse* which had made heavy demands on my time and energy during the middle sixties came out in 1967, which is one explanation why there is so much to talk about between then and 1971: quite simply I had been cocooned by the labour of translation, and now I had to catch up with myself again. The emergence from the muse-darkness, the break with modernism and the writing of the Gifts were a product of this freedom to grow.

In 1971 I started a relationship with my future wife Lesley. Being married and having children in Welsh Wales was a different ballgame to what I'd known before, and inevitably led to new kinds of poetic opportunity and commitment.

THE POET'S AUDIENCE

Poets generally have three kinds of audience: those who form their personal circle, those who go to their public readings, and those who read their work in books, anthologies or magazines. I shall call them the poet's tribal, feudal and commodity audiences respectively, for the sake of convenience and because the terms suggest the relations of production that are involved in each case; not because they are strictly accurate or necessarily exclusive of each other. XYZ may have poems printed to sell to her personal circle; or some who go to ABC's readings may be his friends. A poetry reading is often the way DEF's books are promoted as commodities; and so on. But though there are overlaps, in general the classes are clear.

*   *   *

To take the last first. The commodity audience is the poet's 'market.' There are whole books written on how to market your poems. As a young poet, you are made to feel that the market is the only measure of success and the only way your work will become known. If you fail to have poems published in 'prestigious' magazines or books brought out by the right publishers, your career will be a flop. And indeed, this is largely true. Even your personal circle will begin to doubt your importance if you do not publish in the right places; certainly you will not be invited to poetry readings or Arfon Foundation courses unless you are known as a marketable poet.

The market therefore operates as a filter. It very largely determines whether you can legitimately call yourself a poet. It also claims to have near-absolute power over your immortality. Despite the examples of Gerard Hopkins and Emily Dickinson, neither of whom published anything, and despite the fact that dead books are now as numerous as the sands of Egypt, the myth of the book as the only currency to cross Lethe persists. If you have no book to offer the Boatman your work will not survive and you will surely be forgotten.

Historically, the novel is wholly a product of the market — it does not make sense except as a commodity; and the same is very largely true of our kind of drama, miracle and mumming plays notwithstanding. The box office is the criterion of success, even if its judgement need not be final. But lyric poetry was acknowledged and enjoyed centuries before it became marketable. John Donne was typical of a long line of poets whose reputation owed nothing to the printed book. His poems were copied by hand by those who wanted to read them. They were collected in a book and published after his death, as a sort of commemoration. The published book was in this case an honorific substitute for the manuscript, which incidentally could be sold as a commodity and therefore reach a wider audience. Virtually the whole body of Welsh poetry before the eighteenth century owed its survival to people collecting it in manuscripts for their own personal enjoyment.

Anthologies like *Tottel's Miscellany* were the first books of lyric poetry to be marketed; but, before that, individual lyrics were printed as broadsides and sold at fairs. The anthology persists and is probably still the way most readers come into contact with verse; but the broadside has gone. Individual poems still find their market in odd corners of magazines, so in a sense the magazine has replaced the ballad-seller. The broadside's bigger brother, the chapbook, is very much still with us in the local poetry society publication, in the hand- duplicated, stapled pamphlet, and even, at a more elevated level, in the prestigious poetry magazine itself, Arts Council subsidy and all.

Anthology, broadside and chapbook were in principle merely ways of distributing lyrics. The lyric itself was still not composed as a commodity; at least not in the highbrow world. At a popular level, of course, thousands of 'ballads' were written for the broadside market and eventually enjoyed a precarious immortality as folksongs. But these were despised by the real poets of the day. Even a bourgeois like Donne did not write lyrics as commodities.

The sonnet sequence was the first collection of lyric poetry to be designed from the start as a publishable book. Sidney's *Astrophel and Stella* was clearly a book, not simply an ad hoc collection of sonnets. From now on, the book of poems, the commodity, will be as important in literature as the single lyric inspiration. Herbert's *The Temple*, Blake's *Songs of Innocence and Experience*, Wordsworth and Coleridge's *Lyrical Ballads 1798* or Housman's *The Shropshire Lad* are more than the sum of their parts. Each of them was deliberately designed by their authors as a commodity. This is in spite of the fact that the books are very different from each other, in ideological purpose, presentation and style; in spite of the fact also that a reader will still tend to read individual poems one at a time, not the whole book cover to cover. But the more you can get readers to think of the book and not the single poem, the better publishers are pleased. Publishers sell books, they don't sell poems.

A number of consequences follow from this. There was a time when a poet could just call his collection 'Poems', 'More Poems', 'Further Poems' and (posthumously) 'Last Poems.' This eminently sensible procedure won't do these days: you have to think up snazzy titles to differentiate your product clearly from anyone else's. 'Standing a beer to Michael Schmidt' — if your book is not published by his press — or 'Hello, England', 'Bog rats', 'The Unforeseen Consequences of a Daisy-Wheel', 'BaM bAm BaM', 'Blue Prints for Betelgeuse' . . . As with all advertising, the intention is not seriously to mislead; but that is certainly the effect. One gets seduced by the title into wondering what on earth the poet is up to. Of course, in the vast majority of cases he or she is not up to anything. The poems are just poems — in one or other of the conventional modes that have been prevalent in English verse for the past three decades or so.

Second, what the publisher is after is a homogenised product. He does not want a collection of good poems in twelve different styles. Poor man, he can't advertise his wares as telling a gripping romance, or giving a true picture of life in a Vietnamese paddy-field, or the correct way to catch hummingbirds for dinner. Most people have enough acquaintance with poetry not to believe him if he does. What he decides is sellable is the poet's style, which is rechristened his 'voice.' Miss Hermione Poott is 'the new voice we've all been waiting for'. 'The genuine voice of the working class.' 'A voice to remember.' And so on. The young poet is encouraged to think that his job consists in finding his own individual voice, and once he has found it (and the test is whether he gets published by the right publishers) to stick to it like a limpet. It is his most valuable possession, only to be jettisoned under the most extreme conditions, like changing his religion or going to live in Tierra del Fuego. Of course, in the vast majority of cases the 'voice' is in no wise different from one or other of the conventional styles that have whispered out at us from English verse for the past three decades.

As the poetry market grows and shrinks (but chiefly shrinks) the publisher himself moves more and more into the limelight. A Faber poet, after all, is a Faber poet. But one of the more insidious aspects of this is that the publisher begins to think of himself as an impresario. The poet hands over to him a mass of lyrical material, poems, fragments, what have you. The kindly publisher then *creates* out of this a book of poems that will grace his list. The publisher thus fulfils himself as an artist and the poet is relieved of the onerous task of preferring one poem to another. Everyone knows (don't they?) that poets are the worst judges of their own work. It gets to the point where some publishers are said not to publish anything they can't meddle with first, leaving some pieces out, changing the order of those that are left. And after all, publishers have a lot of experience to draw on. They can see the wood for the trees.

One's only doubt is, what wood?

> And sang within the bloody wood
> When Agamemnon cried aloud . . .

It was doubtless right for Pound, *il miglior fabbro*, to edit 'The Wasteland' for Eliot. I am not sure of the propriety of (say) Cary Archard of Seren Books claiming this privilege for every poet he publishes. Would he create *Paterson* or *The Anathemata* or *Brigg Flats* by this *miglior fabrication?* It is a safe bet that he would not. A publisher aims at a book of self-contained pieces that like the windowless monads of Liebniz all contain the same universe from slightly different aspects. Wherever you open the book you find the guaranteed product, the 'voice', homogenised and clean.

The poet's abdication of formal responsibility to his publisher is only an extreme example of a censorship that runs everywhere in commodity publishing. Readers, we are told, don't like notes. The poem must be self-sufficient. Equally, it must not rely on esoteric knowledge—and what knowledge is not esoteric these days? No matter how difficult his work, the poet must not ease the reader's path, except possibly by giving a clue in the title or a coy little epigraph. Anything else will 'serve as a substitute for the poem' in the reader's mind, and is therefore forbidden. Also the poem itself must not convey too many facts or ideas—that is lecturing the reader, and again is not tolerated. It has to be assumed that if the reader was in the situation described in the poem, he would have the same experience. A vast amount of effort therefore has to go into notating the situation in all its sensory richness. Oddly (from a philosophical point of view) sensation is felt to be more public than thought or emotion, and more immediately accessible to the new reader.

The publisher is not the only danger that the poet must meet if he attempts to market his wares. There is also the malice or stupidity of reviewers. The poetry market as it shrinks has developed extraordinary means of self-preservation. It used to be said that you could take an ordinary liberal Britisher, put him on the Union-Castle boat to South Africa and by the time the ship docked he would be spouting racialism like a fully-fledged colonial. So it is with reviewers. It is hard work adequately to review even one book of poems; and magazines expect their critics to do them in batches. That is part of the trouble, but by no means all of it. Any market looks after its own. In the big world the regional markets of Europe developed the whole panoply of nation states, with their own armies and foreign policy, to protect their values and territories from competitors and potential rivals. The big markets internalised this protection as patriotic fervour. As we know, it was a force strong enough to make four million men die in the trenches of the First World War. The poetry reviewer's determination to resist boarders is a microcosm of this lemming-like patriotism.

The poet may have thought that a few notes would help the reader along; immediately he creates an excuse for the reviewer not to read his poems. He is accused of being an academic snob, of trying to outdo 'The Waste Land.' Or the poet has tried to evade the usual publisher's network and had his work published by a small press, let us say the Platypus Press from Wolverhampton that uses 'unconventional' methods like stapling a booklet together. He is either treated to a delightfully witty discourse on the survival of monotremes (egg-laying mammals) in the English midlands, or gruffly given to understand that if his work was worth publishing at all, it was worth publishing properly.

* * *

If we turn now to the 'feudal' audience at poetry readings, a very different picture emerges. The poet is face to face with people, for a start. He has to entertain a group (or sometimes a crowd, if he is famous enough). His personality has to charm, cajole, dominate or hypnotise these good folk into listening to what his poems are saying. It is a very much more 'natural' medium for the poet, particularly if he is anything of a showman or a performing artist. (A good many poets are not, of course, and in proper feudal societies the poet did not usually recite his work himself but handed it over to a minstrel who recited or sang it for him; but some poets, even so, operated as minstrels as well.)

Poets vary immensely in how they do readings. Very few just read. Listening to poems is quite hard work, and if the poet is not careful, he will overtax our concentration and his poems end up as a gabble for us. R.S. Thomas is very austere in this respect. He rarely chats to the audience between poems; on the other hand, the slowness of his delivery and the fairly long pauses between poems let them breathe in our minds. He has learnt from pulpit and altar how to make serious words reach home.

Some spacing of poems, however, is usually required, to rest the audience's attention. We are often given anecdotes about how this or that poem came to be written. Sometimes the poet tells us what ideas were in his mind. He may even paraphrase the poem for us before he reads it. Variety of approach is desirable. If he has talked about three poems in a row before reading them, he may startle us by launching into the fourth without any introduction at all. There is really only one requisite: to put the audience at their ease in the presence of poetry, so that it speaks to them as only poetry can.

In this respect the poem that is read at a public reading is quite different from the commodity poem you find in books or magazines. There is no taboo on the poet explaining it, even in the middle of a line. Allusions can be notated, background shared with the audience. There is no necessity for the poems to be isolated from the prose world. In fact the opposite is generally true. The audience demands to know the poet, at least to share with him his own interest in his work. In some readings the poems occur as special incidents in an hour of chat.

I remember that when Ted Hughes read from *Crow* in Bangor, he introduced it with a long description of the plot he had started with. The poems, as far as I remember what he said, were fragments of a much larger metaphysical scenario. I have never seen this spiel in print, but I don't imagine that Hughes invented it for our benefit in Bangor. It totally altered the way the poems came over to us. Presumably the censorship and decorum of commodity poetry made it impossible for him to append it to *Crow* as a book of poems; but at a poetry reading he felt free to share it with us.

I call this a 'feudal' audience because the relation of the poet to the group is not unlike a feudal one. Although one usually pays for a ticket — and therefore there is a box office or commodity relationship in the background — the poet is not being paid out of the box office but out of patronage. He would get his fee if no one at all turned up. More important, he relates to the group on a naked power basis. He has to impose his vision on us for an hour or so, unmediated by market forces. If he fails, usually the worse that can happen is we get bored; but in theory we could hiss or rend him limb from limb. It is a personal relationship, like that between a lord and his serfs. The difference between our thralldom to the poet's presence and our market freedom to stop buying his books is comparable to that between the physical unfreedom of the serf and the hypothetical freedom of the wage-earner to choose another job.

I don't want to press this analogy too far: the feudal epithet is more a convenient one than anything else. But the resemblances between the sort of poetry that is successful at poetry readings — and even more, the sort of poetry that is written specifically for readings — and the poetry of the feudal minstrels is worth remarking on. Both tend to be entertainment art above all. Commodity poetry, one might think, is a kind of entertainment too, like buying a cheap novel to read. But in fact one buys a book of poems almost always as a collector of cultural objects. A commodity poem is a fetish, a talisman to sensibility, a thing one owns: much more like a consumer durable than a chance of a quick thrill. That is why it must not be cluttered with mere chat, notes or biographical details.

The poet who reads in public, like the minstrel, is an entertainer. He will sometimes rely on beauty to charm us, but beauty does not hold the attention for very long. Anecdotes and stories are part of his stock in trade; and of course, satire and wit. Some poets resort to trick poems, like reciting at immense speed a bus timetable. If he knows people in the audience he will engage in desultory conversation with them as part of his act—anything that gives him purchase to shift our inertia and win us over.

In general you don't remember individual poems from a reading; but sometimes memorability is part of the effect. People who heard my 'Elegy for the Welsh Dead in the Falklands' obviously remembered it, even more than if they had read it themselves in a magazine. So that sometimes a reading does give you a cultural talisman, as much as a book does. There are no rules in the matter. There are also no critics and reviewers of poetry readings tend to be pretty primitive creatures, like drama critics in the tabloids. They are also thin on the ground and very easily ignored.

*   *   *

The 'tribal' audience is the simplest and most natural for a poet — as opposed to a novelist, for whom his personal circle is largely an embarrassing irrelevance or at most a source of copy. If a poet is writing for a group he knows, he can assume a lot of common interests. Poems will arise from, and then be part of, a continuing conversation. He will read his poems to his friends, or get them to read them to him (which is better), and they can ask him what he means or he can venture information, as the need arises. He is likely to take account of any criticism they offer, for it is on a one-to-one basis, and he can generally trust it to be without malice. The poems become an important part of the life of his community, enjoyed and discussed even when the poet is not present: they have a communal status, like a performance by an amateur dramatic society. He is not a 'writer' so much as a local functionary, like a headmaster, a vicar or even a social worker.

The difference is, these days, in the kind of tribe he belongs to. Poets quite often have only a few friends scattered up and down the country. Their 'tribe' has dispersed, and even the remnants of it that are left are not constant enough to be habit-forming. That is, when a poet meets one of his friends he does not expect to meet him or her *as a poet*, but simply as two members of the professional class, for whom it is simply not done to discuss 'shop.' Only in the sixth form or at university is there usually any possibility for a poet to have an extended tribe, other than that of his fellow poets and rivals.

The situation is ameliorated to some extent by 'writers' groups' and 'creative writing classes'. Women poets, in particular, often seem to find confirmation and reassurance by attending consciousness-raising groups of women writers and would-be writers; and then their poems do recover a social function, even if there is a danger of only preaching to the converted.

*   *   *

In the fifties and sixties there was a movement by universities to academise poets. Many prominent writers earned their living as lecturers, both in America and Britain. Others were given (and still are) temporary accommodation as visiting fellows, poets in residence, teachers of creative writing. The Gregynog 'resident artist' — not necessarily a writer — was until recently a survivor of that phase.

English in universities had taken over from Classics as the major Arts department. The great advantage of English in the student mind was that it offered to teach a living culture, not a dead one. Students opted more and more for courses in contemporary writing. At the same time, however, educated people were alienated as never before from modern poetry, which seemed anyway to be dying on its feet. If the students were not to see English poetry as being as dead as Latin or Greek, something had to be done about it.

Here, then, was a new opportunity for poets to develop a quasi-tribal audience. The only problem was, who with—the staff or the students? The dons tended to see their poet as yet another specialist, beavering away in solitude to produce the 'publications' on which his career prospects depended. They were used to studying poetry on the page, safely insulated from the poet's own fleshy and embarrassing presence. And not many of them liked modern poetry anyway — it wasn't their subject.

On the other hand the students, like policemen, were getting younger every year. Though a young poet, like a young lecturer, could for a time be accepted by students as more or less an equal, his real position as part of the gerontocracy that tortured them with examinations would eventually come home to him. And anyway, changing college is traumatic: graduate students moving to do research often suffer agonies of loneliness and self-doubt. Very few poets went back to their own student society: the temptation to fraternise with academics and take on donnish values must have been overwhelming.

It happened that I entered this academic tribal reserve through the back door and for me it worked — at least for ten years or so. I had been a student in Bangor and left the year before John Danby was appointed to the Chair of English. He was one of the greatest tribal chiefs I have ever met, who inspired people either to passionate loyalty or to a distaste amounting to hysteria. When he heard I was unhappy clerking in Chelmsford, he managed to wangle me a job. I returned to college as what amounted to a permanent bard of the place. I was given a pittance of a salary, and asked if I would mind giving a few first-year tutorials. I was then left to get on with it. It was a perfect set-up for a poet who did not know how to conduct his career.

My flat became a meeting-place for all manner of students, artists, science research workers, folksingers . . . The emphasis shifted year by year. At one time it was the students in Church Hostel and their girl friends who preoccupied me; at another a wildly improbable set of botanists.

When the Welsh Committee of the Arts Council gave me a prize, I wrote to Christopher Davies the Welsh publishers and asked them, if I was willing to sell 300 copies, would they publish the prize-winning book for me. Not unnaturally they said yes — Welsh publishers like printing books, not publishing them, and I was relieving them of the responsibility. So I began to collect names. Some of my friends took five or ten copies apiece, to sell to their friends. Even so, it seems to me extraordinary that we managed to shift 350 copies of a hardback book at 7/6 (thirty-seven and a half new pence, but at least £4.50 at today's prices) in a college of just under eight hundred students. In one woman's hostel of twenty-odd students I sold forty-five copies.

For my subsequent six or seven books and about fifteen pamphlets I dispensed with a commercial publisher altogether and sold them more or less at cost price. I hardly ever sold less than two hundred of anything. If it was a market situation at all — and I suppose that technically it was — it was an extremely local one. It felt more like busking than anything else. I had a great aptitude for begging. Now that I'm respectable I have fewer opportunities to beg, and I fear atrophy has set in; but as a young man, I was very good at it.

But this busking of books was in fact only the tip of the iceberg. Those who came to my flat would ask what I'd been writing, or if they did not I would show them anyway. One poem, 'The Mountain,' took a month to write. During that time everyone would drop in to read the latest instalment. If a singer wanted a new song to sing, or someone wanted a present for a girl, they could come to me. My poems would start arguments, and sometimes settle them too. John Danby liked reading them: he was a marvellous if somewhat self-indulgent reader who could make a poem reverberate through you. He would declare oracularly that I was much better than Yeats. If your professor of English says that sort of thing in public, most undergraduates will take it with a pinch of salt; but even so, you couldn't tell with

Danby — not even when you realised that he didn't like Yeats and mocked at him whenever he could.

One might have expected, in such a *milieu*, that my poems would become mere social chitchat, but in fact the reverse happened. People would come to me full of worries or love-affairs or neurosis, and I would listen carefully and lead them down into themselves, with poetry or music or just picking up the symbolism of what they said; and they would feel peaceful and important to themselves again. Particularly I attended to their dreams — I could very often know them best through what they dreamt about. I suppose I qualified as a guru, though I have to say, not a very respectable one.

It was out of this precarious peace that I made my poems. It was also what they fed into. The 'tribalism' in which I worked was a protected environment. The competition sacred to capitalism was simplified among students to a set of exams to decide what degree they got. But in the sixties, before University expansion really took hold, the vestigial tradition of 'college' as a period isolated from the world was still strong. Students were not plagued by economic worry. They could leave their careers till after they'd finished their degree. Not many students had gramophones or radios; none had televisions, and very few had cars. This made for a compact, self-absorbed community that had time and moral space to create or absorb civilized values.

Of course, it could not last. John Danby, who was an administrator's nightmare — his first act starting a tutorial was to pick up a letter from the mountain of unopened correspondence on his desk, glance at it and consign it ritually to the waste paper basket — in a weak, empire-building moment persuaded the senate that the English department needed a second Chair. Having appointed Alun Jones to the job, he then disappeared to Texas as a visiting professor for a year. I think he rather fancied himself as the Duke in *Measure for Measure*, going into hiding and leaving others to clear out the mess.

Jones said that he found English at Bangor a cottage industry and left it big business. I was first aware of the man and his business when he called me to his office. His first words were, 'I am glad you're in the Department, Tony, but you must realise that if you were not, I could get another lecturer.' A few weeks later my Penguin came out and it got glowing reviews. We heard no more of the hypothetical lecturer, but I realised that my days as a tribal poet were numbered.

When Danby came back from Texas wearing a ten-gallon hat virtually the entire student body met him at the station and escorted him back to college; but it was the last time for the tribe to gather. As Danby said to me once, after the death of his friend Charles Mowatt, Professor of History, 'Now there's only me left. When I go, the rats will have it.'

THE POEM AS SYMPHONY

The idea of a long poem haunts our minds. The great epic narratives of the past are a reproach to us. We require our 'encyclopaedic forms' (to use a phrase of Northrop Fry) to deliver us from the scatter of lyric moments, the divorce of the individual sensibility from what is public and social. But to a large extent the epic function has been usurped by the novel and its part-inheritor the film. Why then bother with long poems?

I cannot answer, save by pointing to what we recover from our failures to write them. The salvaged treasure we get from Keats' *Hyperion* fragments or the individual 'poems' that are stitched together in Wordsworth's *Prelude* or juxtaposed so helplessly in Pound's *Cantos* are of a different order to what we find in great novels. *War and Peace* may be greater than *The Triumph of Life*, but in no sense does it supersede Shelley's poem. Even a novel in verse is a different kind of animal to an epic, however fragmentary.

Neither are these 'fragments' just short poems gone wrong, as Poe posited. They occupy the epic stage, however brief and insecure their pomp. Though there is a gradation between lyric and bits of epic, so that in the abstract we are not sure of the distinction, when we are actually on the border it is usually clear enough which side is which. 'Lines written a few miles above Tintern Abbey' has been called 'a *Prelude* in little'; but if we actually compare it with the childhood episodes from that poem, for example, we see the difference. One is personal statement about experience, a blank verse ode or 'conversation piece' comparable to the rhymed odes of the time; the other is heroic poetry about the youthful deeds of the Romantic hero, that is, the Poetic Imagination itself. It is like comparing the 'Ode on the Morning of Christ's Nativity' with *Paradise Lost*.

It is in this sense that *The Waste Land* can be called a short epic, whereas 'Gerontion' stays well this side of dramatic lyric.

The failure to create epic narratives has been endemic in our culture at any rate since the eighteenth century. None of the examples cohere as epic forms, in the way that *The Divine Comedy* or *Paradise Lost* cohere—that is, not by reference to any set of neo-classical rules derived from Homer, but simply as works of art with epic range. *The Prelude*, for example, though it may seem to have the simple coherence that pertains to any autobiography (because it all happens to one man) is in fact a hotch-potch of episodes, with various formal devices to connect them into a continuous narrative. What is more, these devices often lead away from the formal unity of the work as a whole, as with the question, 'Was it for this?' that introduces the childhood scenes in Book I. To explain what 'this' is, Wordsworth has to invent a purely factitious prologue to his work, about his early plans for epic narratives and his frustration when he found he could not write them. If it is not actually lying to the reader, it is at least not relevant to the poem he was writing. It is clumsy patching and botchwork, no more.

What we have is a set of epic 'idylls'—some quite long—about a hero, Wordsworth's own imagination, as a young boy, as a youth in Cambridge and London, as a young revolutionary in France and as a romantic poet in the West Country. These are in themselves quite sufficient to establish Wordsworth as the major epic poet of his age; but the question of epic form is quite unanswered by his example. Keats, again, working from the other direction, failed to write the evolutionary epic that his two 'Hyperion' fragments promise.

The empiricist basis of the Romantic imagination—the insistence on being true to experience—made any epic form problematic. Epics have to be planned, like a rationalist's universe; and the nearest the true empiricist can get to this is the discovery of a 'pattern in the carpet' after the event. Keats said:

> A Man's life of any worth is a continual allegory—and very few eyes can see the Mystery of his life—a life like the Scriptures, figurative . . .
> (Letter to George and Georgiana Keats, Feb 14—May 3, 1819)

he does not say, figurative of what. The more you plan your allegory—or your epic—the less true it will be to the moment of truth, the experience which your epic is supposed to be about.

Of course, the problem affected other forms too, as D.H. Lawrence's defence of free verse in lyric will testify:

> ... in free verse we look for the insurgent naked throb of the instant moment ... The utterance is like a spasm, naked contact with all influences at once. It does not want to get anywhere. It just takes place.
> ('Poetry of the Present' in *The Complete Poems*, Penguin Books, 1977, p. 185)

But lyric has always been bounden (at least in theory) to the spontaneity of the moment: it was in epic that 'truth to experience' was most fatal, because the Romantic epic hero was the imagination itself, the mystery like a spasm, that 'just takes place.' If there was a plan—and most Romantics felt that there was, and that the poet was a favoured person—it was not the poet's own. Nature, or some such goddess, was responsible, not you. The novel escaped this curse because it still remained a made thing, not just a way of registering what the imagination did and saw.

No epic poem, as opposed to epic poetry, 'just takes place.' We have then a basic dichotomy (as it were, between content and form) at the root of Romantic epic. Either you pursued the form, in which case the anarchic content would sooner or later erupt and destroy your poem from the inside (*Hyperion*), or you pursued the will o'the wisp of imagination and then cobbled together a form for it afterwards (*The Prelude*).

It is important to realise that trusting to the freewheeling imagination (as Keats tried to do in *Endymion*) can produce perfect works of art in the short term. Lawrence's *Birds, Beasts and Flowers* or *The Eve of St Agnes* of Keats are neither of them quite innocent of cultural forms; but they mainly owe their force and beauty to the sense we have that the utterance is like a spasm—it does not want to get anywhere. It just takes place. But epic poetry does seem to want to get somewhere: Aeneas has to get from Troy to Carthage to Italy not simply because the story says he did but because Virgil's real theme is Rome. Adam and Eve have to be driven from paradise in order that Christ may regain it. Spenser tells us about *The Faerie Queene*:

> The generall end therefore of all the boke is to fashion a gentleman or noble person in vertuous and gentle discipline.
> (Letter to Raleigh, *Poetical Works*, Oxford Standard Authors, p. 407)

Wordsworth knew that epics get somewhere, which is why he called his poem 'The Prelude;' but that was merely postponing the formal problem to be resolved in a further poem which he was never able to write. Ezra Pound also seems to have written *The Cantos* in the same touching faith that the form would all come right in the end, and to have been similarly disappointed when coherence never came.

Epic poets, however, do not only write epics. Traditionally they cut their milk teeth on pastorals or 'eclogues.' This is because of the symbolic weight that shepherds have carried from Greek and Hebrew culture into our own, as rulers, religious leaders ('I am the Good Shepherd') and poets. A poet whose topic is one or other facet of human greatness has therefore in the small world of the shepherd a ready-made toy of his material. (Wordsworth could not use this toy world because he took shepherds seriously as shepherds, heroes in their own right, as in 'Michael.')

Another kind of poem that the epic poet could write, beside his usually rather stiff approximations to lyric (as in Milton's sonnets), was the sequence of Georgics, whose purpose is supposedly pedagogic. Virgil's are a textbook on farming, beekeeping and the like; but if there are beekeepers who learn how to harvest honey from Virgil, I have yet to hear of them. The subject of the Georgics is actually some aspect of the Good Life, and the pedagogic instruction is as much a toy as the shepherd's crook in the pastoral. The greatest Georgics in English are Thomson's *Seasons* which don't actually teach you a trade at all. Isaac Newton's science had created an imaginative world which Thomson used epic verse to explore. The enormous optimism that descends to such scrupulous observation of the countryside makes his work, if not epic, at least a worthy occupation for an epic poet. Wordsworth's 'Excursion' has something of the same pseudo-pedagogic motivation; but what spoils it as a Georgics is that it takes its pedagogues (the Pedlar, the Solitary, the Country Parson) too solemnly. They become heroes in their own right, like his shepherds. 'Michael' succeeds because it is after all a very moving poem about a shepherd; but no such reality inheres in the endless discussions these personae of the poet have with one another. Milton never wrote a Georgics, but in some ways the masque 'Comus' has a Georgics' role in his preparation for epic. It has a similar pseudo-pedagogic function and a similar element of serious play. And like the Georgics its subject matter is essentially the good life.

* * *

There are, however, other models for a long poem available to us, apart from epic, georgics and verse novel. Instrumental music in the eighteenth century had created forms which depended on sequences of independent movements that yet complemented one another to build up a single imaginative unity. In the suites and partitas of late baroque, the juxtaposition and variety of moods was like the disposition of panels round an altarpiece. We have a poetic equivalent in Dryden's ode, 'Alexander's Feast; or, the Power of Music,' where each section imitates the effect of Timotheus' lyre as he moves through various moods and emotions. Such a musical format was as yet too tied to lyric to have much to offer the epic imagination; and also, at the baroque level, its contrasts became trivialised as mere display.

In the hundred and fifty years after Dryden, however, two parallel but very different developments in music were to have profound consequences for poetic form. Let me deal with the second first: Schubert's *Lieder* and particularly his Song Cycles, 'Die Schöne Müllerin' and 'Winterreise,' which were themselves a response to contemporary German poetry, demonstrated how a sequence of lyrics could become much greater than the sum of its parts. It could tell a story, uncover psychological drama, make a choreography of moods. The song cycle lies behind many of the lyric sequences of the nineteenth and twentieth centuries, from 'In Memoriam' and 'Maud' to Ted Hughes's 'Crow.' Nor must we forget in Wales the two great sequences of Idris Davies, 'Gwalia Deserta' and 'The Angry Summer.' Not that Ted Hughes or Idris Davies were necessarily conscious of Schubert or his followers—though I think Tennyson certainly was—but that the Song Cycle has constantly cross-fertilised music and poetry and over the years affected our apprehension of both.

The other development was in instrumental music—or mainly so, because sometimes (as in Beethoven's Ninth Symphony or Schoenberg's Second String Quartet) voices were used. To go back to Milton for a second, who of all epic poets was with Dante the most conscious of music. His poem 'At a Solemn Music' begins:

> Blest pair of Sirens, pledges of Heav'ns joy,
> Sphear-born harmonious Sisters, Voice and Verse,
> Wed your divine sounds, and mixt power employ
> Dead things with inbreath'd sense able to pierce,
> And to our high-rais'd phantasie present,
> That undisturbed Song of pure concent,
> Ay sung before the saphire-colour'd throne
> To him that sits theron
> With Saintly shout, and solemn Jubily . . .

Milton sees the combination of poetry and music as reflecting the primal concord of the creation, a reflection that mankind can share,

> As once we did, till disproportion'd sin
> Jarr'd against nature's chime, and with harsh din
> Broke the fair musick that all creatures made
> To their great Lord, whose love their motion sway'd
> In perfect Diapason, whilst they stood
> In first obedience, and their state of good.

Concord is opposed to discord, as obedience is to sin. We have to get in tune with God's purposes again, literally in tune, as in natural tuning, where each interval is solely measured in terms of the overtones or harmonics of the base note. Milton has the early baroque awareness of harmony as belonging to the nature of things.

This awareness was shattered by (of all people!) Johann

Sebastian Bach with his advocacy of equal temperament as a principle of tuning. Notes were deliberately put out of tune slightly in order that a note arrived at from one key should be the same as its counterpart arrived at from another. Thus the G which is the third harmonic (or dominant) of C would be the same as the G which is the fifth harmonic (or subdominant) of D; and so on. In the old days, if your keyboard was tuned in C, then every key sharper or flatter was progressively more out of tune. The key of G major was 'sourer' than C major, and D than G; and similarly with F major, B flat major, E flat major and so on. But on this new principle it does not matter where you start tuning a piano: the notes will have exactly the same tuning wherever you start. Music ceases in principle to be a matter of concord and discord, and becomes an art of modulation and key-change.

The new language was at first put to rather boring uses. The early writers of symphonies were clearly fixated on tonic and dominant chords, repeating them over and over again as one key fought it out with another. This primordial obsession with simple chords hovers on the edge of being boring even in the finale of Beethoven's fifth symphony; but it is a small price to pay for the colossal spiritual drama and formal adventures that the new language made possible, not simply in symphony, quartet and sonata but increasingly in opera and music drama also.

The new forms—symphony, string quartet and sonata—took over from the multi-faceted suites and sonatas of the baroque. They too were in a series of movements (usually a symphony or quartet has four, a sonata three) but instead of the movements being like facets of a single static situation (as in baroque suites) the movements of a symphony are dynamic like different acts of a play: not a drama like Sophocles' 'Oedipus the King' which is only one movement of the imagination from beginning to end, but something like Shakespeare's 'Winter's Tale' or all three parts of Aeschylus's 'Oresteia' trilogy.*

---

* There are one-movement symphonies but they evolved secondarily—as indeed the single Sophoclean play might well have done in Greek drama, if the trilogy was originally the norm.

Consider 'The Winter's Tale.' It starts with a long agonised tragic movement about the insane jealousy Leontes has about his wife's quite innocent affection for his own childhood friend. It actually takes more or less three acts to work out, but it is all one movement of the imagination, briefly interrupted by a vision of calm as a messenger describes the oracle at Delphi.

The second movement is very short, a kind of bizarre scherzo where Leontes' baby daughter is put ashore in a strange country but the lord who has saved her from his jealous rage is killed: 'exit, pursued by a bear'; the baby is found by shepherds who don't know who she is.

The third movement could be described as a *pastorale*, a pastoral festival, with a short prelude by Time to tell us that sixteen years have passed. The baby is now a girl who falls in love with an incognito prince. The prince's own father (who is the friend Leontes was jealous of) turns up and threatens to punish everyone concerned; but a nobleman lets them escape.

The fourth movement shows Leontes suffering from remorse for having (as he thinks) murdered his wife and daughter. Into this penitential scene come the lovers, hotly pursued by the prince's father. The play is resolved by a 'statue' of the supposedly dead queen coming to life again, the girl is recognised as her daughter, and everyone lives happily ever after.

The scheme is very typical of symphonic construction—indeed, why no one ever wrote a Winter's Tale Symphony is a puzzle, it fits so well. Each movement reflects a central tragic situation—not jealousy as such, but the way age and experience pervert youth's love and innocence and yet are redeemed by them. Each movement is quite different from the others in mood and formal organisation, and yet each is part of a larger whole where alone it finds its true meaning and purpose.

Music is a mysterious art, and always has been. I think few people are really very aware of key changes as they happen in the course of a piece of music. We can sometimes tell when a tune returns in a key different from its first appearance; but even that is hard work. Most of the time these necessary bones of the symphony operate for us in an entirely subconscious way, like the laws of perspective in post-renaissance painting or the rules of English grammar in a piece of prose. But key-changes are not therefore any less crucial to what is happening. Without them there would be no symphony; the string quartet would still be limited to the equivalent of Purcell's fantasias.

Key-changes make possible not just the drama and tension within a symphonic movement, but also (in a mysterious fashion) the way the movements of a symphony add up to a whole; the way they lean on each other, answer each other, fulfil their destiny only in the company of each other. They correspond in some obscure way to whatever it is that gives shape to 'The Winter's Tale' in all its heterogeneous variety: not just the plot, but a sense of design that seems a revelation of how things are.

Symphonic music based on key change obviously impressed poets. There is talk of poetry 'aspiring to the condition of music.' T.S. Eliot called some of his early poems 'Preludes' and the climax of his work was 'Four Quartets.' 'The Waste Land' itself was supposed to derive its structure from musical example. It is probable, nevertheless, that it was not the underlying key structure that appealed to the poets. What they imitated was, first, the division into very different movements without obvious narrative connection, but nevertheless building into a whole greater than the sum of its parts; second, the way phrases were used as motifs and themes in an abstract tapestry of sound and meaning; and third, an emphasis on the resonance and development of those phrases, rather than any discursive exposition.

The application of these 'symphonic' principles to medium length poems like 'The Waste Land' or 'Ash Wednesday,' despite the dangers of obscurity, works very well. I remain unconvinced that they succeed on a much larger scale. Even in music itself there is a cut-out point: after an hour even the most organised symphony starts to sound long. Wagner's application of symphonic principles to three or four-hour music dramas relies on extra-musical organisation—the story-line, the characters, the scenery—as much if not more as on the interweaving of musical leitmotifs. And when poetry imitates symphonic music it does so in a very impressionistic way, lacking the deeper organisation of key that holds a real symphony together. There is a danger of formlessness and consequent boredom if the structure is too extended.

Nevertheless, we can isolate in modern poetry a kind of poetry that we can call 'symphonic'—in this loose, impressionistic sense; and some of these poems, moreover, are among the central poetic achievements of our century, the counterpart of the epic and georgics of the past. Here is a short list, besides the Eliot pieces already mentioned:

>W.B. Yeats: 'Easter, 1916'
>Hart Crane: 'The Bridge'
>Federico García Lorca: 'Llanto por Ignacio Sánchez Mejías'
>Basil Bunting: 'Briggflatts'
>Allen Ginsberg: 'Howl'
>Ken Smith: 'Fox Running'

Sometimes they veer to lyric, sometimes to epic. In fact, it is typical of the symphony, both in music and in poetry, to mix genres—sometimes in an extreme way, as nursery rhyme with elegy. Even 'Easter, 1916' shows us several different kinds of poetry—the rather discursive social description contrasted with the refrain:

>All changed, changed utterly.
>A terrible beauty is born—

then the passage about the heart as a stone in the stream, an extended epic simile that works as a symbolist poem in its own right; and then the final passionate questioning and invocation of the dead. 'Easter, 1916' (partly because its metre stays the same throughout) is ambiguous as to genre. It can easily be construed as extended lyric—we may not feel that symphony is a relevant or necessary description. But the sense of separate movements is very strong. Also typical of the symphony is the supra-personal awareness. It has an epic dimension, in that it concerns a society face to face with its destiny. In Lawrence's phrase, it does not 'just take place.' It wants to get somewhere. 'I write it out in a verse'—

the writing of the poem is a performative use of words, an act of endorsement—

> MacDonagh and MacBride
> And Connolly and Pearce
> Now and in time to be,
> Wherever green is worn,
> Are changed, changed utterly:
> A terrible beauty is born.

One thinks of Eliot's 'These fragments I have shored against my ruin' or even Milton's endorsement of his theme in the opening invocation of *Paradise Lost*, or Virgil's 'Arma virumque cano'— 'Arms and the man I sing—that man who was to suffer so much—

> dum conderet urbem,
> Inferretque deos Latio

until he should found a city and bring gods to Latium. The poem is an endorsing act, whether of Rome or Paradise or the terrible beauty of Irish freedom, or even of the imagination's need to stay alive in the Wasteland of modern Europe. That performative act is what epic hands on to the symphony. Cano. Sing, heavenly muse. I write it out in a verse.

'Easter, 1916' is symphony at its closest to lyric; if we turn to Lorca's lament for the bullfighter Ignacio Sánchez Mejías the symphonic aspect has moved more into focus. For one thing, the four sections of the poem are widely different in rhythm and style. The terrifying percussive beat of the opening movement is suggestive of Stravinsky's 'Rite of Spring,' but more tragic, more like a dirge—

> *A las cinco de la tarde.*
> *Eran las cinco en punto de la tarde . . .*
> *Un ataúd con ruedas es la cama*
> *a las cinco de la tarde.*
> *Huesos y flautas suenan en su oído*
> *a las cinco de la tarde.*
> *El toro ya mugía por su frente*

> *a las cinco de la tarde.*
> *El cuarto se irisaba de agonía*
> *a las cinco de la tarde . . .*

> At five in the afternoon.
> It was exactly five in the afternoon . . .
> A coffin on wheels is his bed
> At five in the afternoon.
> Bones and flutes rung in his ears
> At five in the afternoon.
> Now the bull bellows on his forehead
> At five in the afternoon.
> The room became irredescent with agony
> At five in the afternoon . . .

The second movement moves into a world of dream imagery punctuated by a refrain '*Que no quiero verla!*'—'I do not want to see it!' It is in the ballad octosyllabics of the *Romancero Gitano*, moving into longer lines as it swells into praise of Ignacio's prowess and beauty. The third section is more meditative—quatrains of long lines as the poet takes in the physical reality of the death; and the fourth moves into the nobility of high lament:

> *No te conoce nadie. No. Pero yo te canto.*
> *Yo canto para luego tu perfil y tu gracia.*
> *La madurez insigne de tu conocimiento.*
> *Tu apetencia de muerte y el gusto de su boca.*
> *La tristeza que tuvo tu valiente alegría.*

> Nobody knows you. No. But I sing of you.
> I sing for posterity of your profile and your grace.
> The noble maturity of your understanding.
> Your appetite for death and the taste of its mouth.
> The sadness inherent in your valiant gaiety . . .
>   (trans. J.L. Gili)

Again, the performative word, the endorsing act of the poem—'*Pero yo te canto*'—'But I sing of you.' Ignacio's heroic beauty and courage is not simply a personal possession, it is the ideal of his people:

> *Tardará mucho tiempo en nacer, si es que nace,*
> *un andeluz tan claro, tan rico de aventura . . .*
>
> Not for a long time will be born, if ever,
> an Andalusian so noble, so rich in adventure.

Lorca's *Llanto* is still intensely lyrical, but in its symphonic frame it has appropriated many of the functions of epic, the song of heroic deeds with claim on the imagination of a people, which is endorsed by the poet in the act of singing it. Symphonic structures can, however, arise from other forms than lyric: from the epic idyll, for example, or the various kinds of ode—including that most exotic and alien of forms (for most Europeans), the Whitmanesque free-verse 'song of myself.' 'The Bridge' by Hart Crane is perhaps such a work, though far more than the others in the short list it tends to break down into a sequence of separate pieces.

For the symphony is to be distinguished from the sequence, whether of lyrics, idylls, elegies or what not. Rilke's 'Duino Elegies' are not symphonic. Each elegy is a separate poem in its own right, in a way that we don't normally feel about the movements of a symphony. But it should be stressed that the independence or not of the several movements, their number, and the relationships between them, have to be peculiar to the work in question: no two symphonies are the same. The difference between a centripetal sequence and a loosely organised symphony will probably remain problematic.

The question arises, is the poem as symphony necessarily in more than one movement? Musical symphonies can be one-movement affairs, for example Sibelius's seventh. Is there anything corresponding to this is poetry? Allen Ginsberg's 'Howl' is certainly symphonic in the sense we are using the term. Technically it has three movements, but I suspect that most readers feel the last two are more postscripts than movements. If a poem has some relation to musical form, however loosely, and if it has supra-personal awareness and complexity of theme, then there is a prima facie case for calling it 'symphonic.' Clearly the symphony shades into other forms. Yeat's Byzantium poems, for example, seem to me as much symphonic as lyric, yet they are shorter than many of his poems that are certainly lyrical. I think we must leave every case to be decided on its merits, according to the context in which we find ourselves.

APPENDIX

When I submitted this book for publication I regarded the following poems as my 'symphonies', and they are referred to as such in subsequent chapters. They fall into two groups, the earlier, shorter ones, and the later, book-length works.

Group I
1   Elegiac Ode (*Formal Poems* 1960)
2   The Bombing of Guernica (*Poems 1951-67*)
3   Day Movements (*Poems 1951-67*)
4   Space (one movement) (*Spirit Level* 1974)
5   Elegy for the Welsh Dead (one movement) (*Blodeuwedd and Other Poems*, 1988)

Group II
6   Castles (*Castles: Variations on an Original Theme* 1993)
7   All Hallows (*All Hallows: Symphony in 3 movements* 1995)

In the light of my subsequent work, however, while I still regard the first five as having symphonic features, I would now (June 1997) limit the term 'symphonies'—works of epic scope but without a continuous epic narrative—to these four:

1   Castles
2   All Hallows
3   A Gwynedd Symphony (not yet published)
4   Suite of Trumps: A Tarot Symphony
        (one movement completed but unpublished)

WAR

Not many Anglo-Welsh poets seem to have been born in the early thirties, compared with the very prolific crop of the twenties or forties. My birth date was 1931. I lived with my grandparents in Liverpool until 1939, when my Welsh grandfather decided that Merseyside was a prime target for the Luftwaffe and the obvious thing was to move back to Wales. He would have liked to return to his native *bro* round Chirk and Llangollen; but my grandmother wasn't having it. They compromised on Colwyn Bay—at least it was in Denbighshire—and bought a largish semi-detached house called Hafod, surrounded by fields waiting to be turned into building sites.

We were expecting war to break out; but at the age of eight I was the first person in the house to know that it had. I happened to be listening to the wireless when Mr Chamberlain announced the fact. I rushed round telling everyone, trying to look solemn but in fact quite excited by having such an important message to deliver. I was also the first person to know that the war was over and went from door to door being rewarded with kisses and joy all down the road.

During my most formative years, therefore, from when I was eight to when I was fourteen, we were at war. True, Colwyn Bay was not much involved in hostilities. There were soldiers, and a large garage turned into a factory for assembling jeeps. During the blitz we used to climb the hill behind us and watch Liverpool burning in the dusk. We had air raid shelters, of course—ours was in the garage, under the house, reinforced by sandbags. When the warning sounded we all put on our siren-suits, so that we looked like a Teddy Bear's picnic, and went down there to lie on campbeds. But it was fairly unexciting, even humdrum, what happened to us. Very few bombs fell anywhere near Colwyn Bay.

All the same, war was unescapable. Families were broken up, refugees shunted from house to house. My cousin and I followed the campaigns with *Daily Telegraph* wall maps. I had a large collection of Ministry of Information books on topics like the Battle of Britain, the Home Guard or the naval war in the

Mediterranean. Particularly were we interested in warships and naval battles: one of my most spectacular investments was a copy of *Janes Fighting Ships* for 1944, which I still have and know most of it by heart. It cost four guineas (£4.20) at a time when my pocket money was maybe a shilling (5p.) a week, from which I was expected to buy my own sweet ration and toys. What is more, as if earth was not enough for the wars going on in our heads, we colonised the planets, made huge maps of them, with lists of their fighting ships, aircraft, governments, weights and measures and so on—we'd inherited a *Whittaker's Almanac* with the house. Being stamp collectors we even made stamp catalogues à la Stanley Gibbons for philatelists of Jupiter and Saturn! All these extra-terrestrial countries were then free to conduct elaborate diplomacy, do trade or make wars with one another.

We also turned the back-garden into a sort of inland sea, where battleships and destroyers roughly made of building planks from down the road used to lurk in enormous harbours of bricks laid end to end between the dying daffodil leaves and the hens that lived behind the summer-house. These ungainly birds conducted their own squawking versions of realpolitik, strutting about like Hitler or Goering. I never liked hens. The smell of their mash and the peculiar whine they affected to do business were a constant accompaniment to the planetary campaigns we waged among the peonies.

John Barnie has suggested* that 'we no longer value the heroic and so do not prepare for situations where its values might be a factor in human dignity.' Whatever might be said about the post-war generation, this was certainly not true of us. The early battles of the Second World War so obviously depended on heroes: there was nothing like the mass slaughter and wastage of heroic potential that you got in the trenches of 1914-18. Before Pearl Harbour, certainly, heroic values were paramount simply because there was nothing to replace them. Malta, our key to the Mediterranean, was defended from attack by three out-of-date bi-

---

* John Barnie: 'Heroic Laughter' in *The King of Ashes* (Gomer, 1989).

plane fighters. The battle to save the army at Dunkirk was surely a heroic (and unprofessional) affair. The Battle of Britain itself was fought by young pilots whose sense of doom was manifest—fought against great odds every bit as dependent on individual nerve and battle skill as Cúchulainn at the ford defending Ulster against the armies of Connacht. The joy in battle was not, perhaps, so expressionistically portrayed as in Irish saga but it was certainly there; as was sadness at killing good men on the other side, and at the same time grief and desire of revenge for friends killed on your own. To say that the fighter pilots were or were not 'trained in the last vestiges of the heroic tradition' seems to me quite meaningless: the whole of Western Europe was resonant with heroic values at that time—often, it is true, wasted by incompetence, dishonesty or the weapons of mass destruction, but never forgotten. It was not merely in the air that we saw them revealed. The battle of the armed merchantman Jervis Bay against a German pocket battleship was as heroic and as doomed as anything in saga.

The beginning of the First World War was essentially a discovery of male togetherness in the trenches, faced with appalling slaughter and a strategical incompetence that made heroism almost meaningless—a discovery that forms the subject-matter of *In Parenthesis* and which was itself overwhelmed in the brutality that followed. But the opening stages of the Second World War were surely quite different as human experience. The Spanish Civil War and the gas-attack on Ethiopia were preludes that made us aware of the evil that was abroad—an evil, be it said, that we participated in ourselves in the later stages: 'total war' is not a heroic idea, nor a moral one. But at the beginning, the Second World War was anything but a revelation of male togetherness. Isolation, fear, boredom, solitary courage were the order of the day. In the First War the generals wantonly wasted the biggest armed might the world had ever seen, by using it in ways where its strength was simply mown down by new weapons; but in the Second the authorities were struggling with military unpreparedness on a scale that seemed to guarantee defeat. They had to save time and resources by strategic withdrawals across the board. At least until Alamein, the Second World War was fought by a rearguard; and as always in rearguards, the hero and the refugee dominated our experience.

Even later, however, the hero was surprisingly relevant to the war. John Barnie mentions the death of a Danish resistance fighter Jørgen Schmidt as if it were a kind of anachronism. The Gestapo finally tracked him down to a villa where he was recuperating from wounds and as they were questioning the woman at the door, Schmidt shot one of them from the top of the stairs. Panic followed, the Gestapo called in troops and the villa was surrounded. Jørgen Schmidt kept them at bay, however, throughout the night until the house began to burn down around him. Finally, according to an eye-witness, the roof caved in and the walls started to collapse:

> Then, suddenly, he charged through the smashed French windows. a wild, slight figure in blue-and-white pyjamas. He rushed out onto the lawn, the Sten-gun at his hip still firing.
>
> He got only a few steps before they cut him down. He looked like a pathetic doll crumpled on the grass.
>
> But he went out as he would have wished—fighting to the last.

Denmark (as John Barnie says) was a special case—occupied rather than conquered, given 'favoured nation' status by the Nazis, where the resistance was small and unpopular. But in other countries the resistance fighters were a sort of norm, however outnumbered by the more or less compromised mass of the population. Barnie tries to draw a distinction between the hero who breaks ranks to gain undying glory for himself in death and (our twentieth century ideal fighter) the *guerillero*, the ambusher, who hits and runs to fight again. I do not think that this distinction will hold, in spite of the guerillero's more obvious sense of having a job to do and his lesser emphasis on dying a glorious death. What about Ché Guevara, a model of a guerillero if ever there was one, who left Castro and the successful revolution in Cuba to die an ignominious yet heroic and (to his admirers) glorious death fighting imperialism in Bolivia?

Anyway, not all heroes die gloriously. In the *Iliad* Hector's death is on the battlefield, but there are elements of the pathetic about it, not simply heroic glory. Agamemnon is killed by his wife's lover when he returns home; and though there is a sense in which he accepts the doom that awaits him—he treads the carpet laid down for him against his better judgement—his actual death is without glory of any kind. Odysseus when he returns finally to Ithaca seems to me a perfect model for the *guerillero*—even to the terrible revenge á la I.R.A. he exacts from the women who have collaborated with the enemy. Eventually even the guerillero looks forward to a heroic and often public denoument. Pierce and Connolly take possession of the Dublin Post Office. The people of Warsaw rise up against the Nazis.

For, conversely, the hero is not solely motivated by desire for glory. Heroic values have an economic and social function in the society where they operate. The hero's job is to defend his society, like Hector or Cúchulainn or Beowulf. Where state-of-the-art military technology is too expensive for any but an *elite*—bronze age armour, Spitfires—the hero is the only one who can wield it. A spitfire pilot's sense of doom is intimately bound up with the precious hardware he drives. It becomes a funeral pyre if he dies, making his death in battle obvious before all people. So with the bronze age or iron age hero: if he falls in battle, his enemies will try and strip his armour from him, his friends will try to save it for his grave. The ultimate connexion between a hero's job and his desire for glory is perhaps given by the Japanese suicide pilots in the last war who became living bombs against American warships. They did so partly to obey their emperor—so did Roland at Roncesvalle—and so fulfil the military requirements of their society; but also, partly, to achieve individual glory for themselves.

But for all his prominence in the early days of the Second World War, the hero was by no means typical. To an extent of course he never is—by definition the hero is an exceptional person. But in the early 1940's it was a case of 'many are called but few are chosen.' And what they were called for—the army clerks, the WAAFs, ship's cooks and wireless operators, the ironically named 'privates,' victims of blanko and bullshit—was largely a matter of boredom, diffused fear and guilt, and the re-education of ordinary decent people into agents of mass destruction. Young English and Welsh poets participated in this calling. The three significant English-language poets of the Second World War from Britain were Alun Lewis, Keith Douglas and Lynette Roberts. Only Keith Douglas in any real sense 'fought':

> Now in my dial of glass appears
> the soldier who is going to die.
> He smiles, and moves about in ways
> his mother knows, habits of his.
> The wires touch his face: I cry,
> NOW. Death, like a familiar, hears
>
> and look, has made a man of dust
> of a man of flesh. This sorcery
> I do. Being damned, I am amused
> to see the centre of love diffused
> and the waves of love travel into vacancy.
> How easy it is to make a ghost.
>
> ('How to kill')

'His sword rang in the heads of mothers . . .' The heroic laughter and excitement of battle has given way to a kind of distanced 'amusement,' as of the damned. This was certainly one way in which the modern intellectual faced the war.

The other two poets reflect a world where war is everywhere yet battle happens rarely and nearly always offstage. This killed Alun Lewis—the waiting, the guilt, the spiritual vaccuum lit by flashes of passion and despair. Above all, perhaps, the irrelevance of what his upbringing had made him to what his function was now. Lynette Roberts's work has not even yet been reprinted or properly assessed. The Second World War was the first in which the distinction between combat area and home was blurred. In Coventry or Swansea, Dresden or Hiroshima, you were as much in the front line as El Alamein or Normandy. In that sense it was a total war. There were quiet sectors, of course; but nowhere was exempt. 'Blighty' was as likely to be a ruined street as anywhere else. 'Tipperary' was not just a long way, it had receded to infinity. Even more was this the case in psychological and social terms.

Lynette Roberts is a war poet moving into this new terrain, angry, domestic, celebratory and satirical. The difficulty of her work, at once modernist and feminine, has not made appreciation easy; but where Douglas and Lewis were tentative and fragmentary, at least as poets—Lewis as a short-story writer is very different—Lynette Roberts achieved in her 'heroic poem' and a handful of lyrics a war poetry that is absolutely sure of itself and totally original. Like most of the other war-poets of the twentieth century (though she, like Sassoon, physically survived) her important work was over by the end of the war she wrote about. She seems to have given up writing altogether in the early fifties.

Poets in the 1914-18 war had perforce shared in the shock of modern war on the naive 'boy-scout' or public-schoolboy patriotism expressed in the sonnets of Rupert Brooke. The satiric aim of Sassoon and Owen had been to destroy this heroic idealism in the name of pity—pity for the human beings crowded together, loving each other as comrades and being killed together in the trenches through the pompous inefficiency of those who were supposed to lead them. This job had been done by poets, and done so well that most liberal people, when they consult their feelings about war, instinctively think of Wilfred Owen. He is for them the war poet *par excellence*. War is something we suffer, something to protest about, not something we do. But poets in the Second World War realised instinctively that their war was not really like that. Rosenberg and Edward Thomas had more to say to their condition than Owen and Sassoon.

But whereas the experience of the trenches was corporate—an all-male community radically different from the larger society at home it was supposed to be defending—the experience of the combatant in the Second World War tended to be individual and fragmentary and much more of a piece with conditions at home. It was rarely all-male for more than a few days. Battle had been the norm in the First War, it was the exception in the Second. Of course, one can easily exaggerate this aspect. There were times and theatres of war where soldiers or sailors fought continuously for months on end; but it was not, even so, the sheer static slog of the trenches. To be a boy following campaigns in the 1939-45 war was exciting because the whole thing was intensely mobile, and new concepts of warfare—commando raids, radar, rockets, atom bombs—were continually being generated. Perhaps something similar to the conditions of 1914-18 persisted in the nightmare of convoys nosing their way across the no-man's-land of the North Atlantic or in the massive destruction of the Russian Front; but on the whole the War was like a boardgame where pieces were waiting to move for most of the time. For an onlooker like me, the game was fast, but for a pawn, it was the waiting, the waste, that remained and killed.

*   *   *

Two things prevented English-language poets from coping in their work with this new experience of war. One was the negative feedback from past ideological developments—not just the Wilfred-Owenlike expectations they inherited from 1918 but the sense of a failed Jehad or holy war in Spain and the confusing abdication of leading writers like Auden from the British scene. The other was this sense of fragmentation and waste. In the circumstances, the most mature British poetic responses to the war were not in the English language but in Scots Gaelic and Welsh.

Somhairle MacGill-eain (Sorley MacLean) of Raasay was already a great poet when he fought in the North African campaigns. His love poems 'to Eimhir' had revolutionised Gaelic literature and given it a wholly modern and wide-ranging poetry of great power. One of the things those poems had turned on was MacLean's failure, for whatever good reasons, to join the fight in Spain with his heroes Cornford and Julian Bell. Now, in Libya, there was no mistake. MacLean's war poems (properly so-called) are few in number, but they cover the whole gamut of battle. He sketches first the detachment of the warrior:

> Far from me the Island
> and every loved image in Scotland,
> there is a foreign sand in History
> spoiling the machines of the mind.

> Far from me Belsen and Dachau,
> Rotterdam, the Clyde and Prague,
> and Dimitrov before a court
> hitting fear with the thump of his laugh.
>
> Guernica itself is very far
> from the innocent corpses of the Nazis
> who are lying in the gravel
> and in the khaki sand of the Desert.

He accepts the struggle as 'not to be avoided': 'the brain's eye is not squinting' and whatever history was like,

> I am of the big men of Braes,
> of the heroic Raasay MacLeods,
> of the sharp-sword Mathesons of Lochalsh;
> and the men of my name—who were braver
> when their ruinous pride was kindled?
>
> 'Going Westwards'

MacLean has available to him a tradition of heroic expectations that would be very problematic nowadays for an English poet. It is like a land he has heard about, but never visited:

> South, south to Bir Hacheim,
> tanks and guns at high speed,
> there was a jump and kick in the heart
>
> and a kind of delight—
> it was the battle joy—
> as one heard in the tale,
> not knowing if it was a lie.
>
> ('South')

But in this case, typically, the 'battle joy' was premature—they had to retire under enemy bombardment before they could 'put a stop to big Rommel'! It is always a mistake to import too much atavism into MacLean—he can undercut it at any moment with an irony that is never simply defensive. Because he derives from Gaelic tradition, with its clan structure, its bitterness at what destroyed it, and its roots in the distant past, it does not mean he is therefore not modern. His poem 'Heroes' begins:

> I did not see Lannes at Ratisbon
> nor MacLennan at Auldearn
> nor Gillies MacBain at Culloden,
> but I saw an Englishman in Egypt.
>
> A poor little chap with chubby cheeks
> and knees grinding each other,
> pimply unattractive face—
> garment of the bravest spirit.

Like Jørgen Schmidt this 'poor little chap' died a hero's death:

> Word came to him in the bullet shower
> that he should be a hero briskly,
> and he was that while he lasted
> but it wasn't much time he got.
>
> He kept his guns to the tanks,
> bucking with tearing crashing screech,
> until he himself got, about the stomach,
> that biff that put him to the ground,
> mouth down in sand and gravel
> without a chirp from his ugly high-pitched voice.

MacLean's description plays down neither the pathetic nor the grotesque—being heroic does not exonerate you from any of the pain or indignity of being human. Yet finally, what comes over in the poem is affection and admiration:

> I saw a great warrior of England,
> a poor mannikin on whom no eye would rest;
> no Alasdair of Glen Garry;
> and he took a little weeping to my eyes.

MacLean's is a mature compassion but also a concern for what is human and admirable. It takes on board both the pity of Wilfred Owen and the satire of Sassoon against the lies of propaganda and ideology. He comes across a dead German soldier in the desert and he thinks of a Nazi saying that the Fuehrer had restored to German manhood 'the right and joy of dying in battle':

> I thought of the right and the joy
> that he got from his Fuehrer . . .
>
> of the pomp and the fame
> that he had, not alone,
> though he was the most piteous to see
> in a valley gone to seed . . .

The poet wonders whether the young man was a Jew-baiter, or just one of the greater band

> led, from the beginning of generations,
> unwillingly to the trial
> and mad delirium of every war
> for the sake of rulers.

It hardly seems to matter now—

> Whatever his desire or mishap,
> his innocence or malignity,
> he showed no pleasure in his death
> below the Ruweisat Ridge.
> ('Death Valley')

The two sides of war—the 'mad delirium' of its destruction of human life, the mendacity and selfishnes of its leaders, and yet its grim opportunity for human greatness—could not be better illustrated than from these two poems. What is strange in them is the warrior's detachment and compassion that sees humanity on both sides of no-man's-land, and yet 'the brain's eye is not squinting' in the struggle that is not to be avoided.

* * *

Perhaps the greatest religious poem in the world, the *Bhagavad Gita*, takes place between two armies drawn up for battle in a civil war. Kinsmen are preparing to kill kinsmen. Arjuna the great warrior tells his charioteer, the god Krishna, to drive their chariot between the drawn-up battlelines. It is what used to be called a reconnaissance raid, to determine where the enemy is putting his strength; but as he contemplates his friends and relatives drawn up on the other side, he gives way to despair:

> My great bow Gandiva falls from my hands, and the skin of my flesh is burning; I am no longer able to stand because my mind is whirling and wandering.
> And I see forebodings of evil, Krishna. I cannot foresee any glory if I kill my own kinsmen in the sacrifice of battle . . .
> These I do not wish to slay, even if I myself am slain. Not even for the kingdom of the three worlds: how much less for a kingdom of the earth!
> If we kill these evil men, evil shall fall upon us: what joy in their death could we have, O Janardana, mover of souls?
> I cannot therefore kill my own kinsmen, the sons of king Dhritarashtra, the brother of my own father. What happiness could we ever enjoy, if we killed our own kinsmen in battle?
> Even if they, with minds overcome by greed, see no evil in the destruction of a family, see no sin in the treachery to friends;
> Shall we not, who see the evil of destruction, shall we not refrain from this terrible deed? ...
> And when Arjuna the great warrior had thus unburdened his soul, 'I will not fight, Krishna,' he said, and then fell silent.

The rest of the poem, formally at least, constitutes Krishna's reply:

> Krishna smiled and spoke to Arjuna—there between the two armies the voice of God spoke these words.

Krishna puts Arjuna's dilemma in the context of eternity, but an eternity much more like that of an imaginative creation, like a poem or a symphony 'which having been must ever be'—than of the Christian tradition's Day of Judgement:

> Because we all have been for all time: I and thou, and those kings
> of men. And we all shall be for all time, we all for ever and
> ever.

If our lives are really like this, like parts of a story or a poem written once and for all in the mind of God, then truly we cannot escape from action by refraining from action. Godhead is found in all of us, living our lives in His wisdom. That is why Krishna says,

> I am the cleverness in the gambler's dice. I am the beauty of all
> things beautiful. I am victory and the struggle for victory. I
> am the goodness of those who are good.
> Of the children of Vrishni I am Krishna; and of the sons of
> Pandu I am Arjuna.
> (trans. Juan Mascaró—Penguin Classics)

Like MacLean's, the 'brain's eye' of the righteous warrior in the struggle that is not to be avoided 'is not squinting;' and though there seems to be a great difference between the Scottish poet's saying,

> I am of the big men of Braes,
> of the heroic Raasay MacLeods,
> of the sharp-sword Mathesons of Lochalsh,

and God saying to Arjuna 'of the sons of Pandu I am Arjuna,' yet they seem to me recognisably part of the same spectrum of feeling. A man has to do what a man has to do.

Or does he? Arjuna in the Gita is not so much answered as overwhelmed—a bit like Job by the Voice out of the whirlwind. But Arjuna's 'I will not fight' demands a different kind of eschatology to Krishna's if it is to make imaginative sense. It may seem strange to oppose Waldo Williams the Welsh pacifist to Sorley MacLean as a great war-poet. Waldo never fought in battle, he never gave countenance to war; when, later on, he realised that the taxes he paid were going towards the war in Korea he resigned from his job (where tax was deducted P.A.Y.E.) and went to prison rather than pay them. Against war he put peace, against the warrior he put the saint, against the sovereignty of the nation he put community and the kinship of all mankind.

Waldo Williams' poetry is astonishingly varied, in form and intention; but at its heart his inspiration is all of a piece. Let us begin neither with his large-scale masterpieces such as '*Y Tŵr a'r Graig*' ('The Tower and the Rock') or '*Mewn Dau Gae*' ('In Two Fields') nor with his more obviously anti-war poems, but with his very last sonnet of all, '*Llandysilio-yn-Nyfed*,' about a village in Welsh-speaking Pembrokeshire where Waldo spent much of his boyhood. The name means 'St Tysilio-in-Dyfed.' Here is the poem:

LLANDYSILIO-YN-NYFED

I am often amazed. What light came from beyond
That to his elect ones Christ could reveal
When life for us was brutal, full of wrong,
Made great by neither purpose nor ideal?
I remember how we'd all go to the door
When the church bell rang for a better year—
Maldwyn's gentleness on Dyfed once more
As the imagination far and near
Travelled deep night. We'd see small companies,
Without exploit of cities, yoke the world one
And among them, salvation clear, we'd see
In the white flame rejoicing for God's son
Tysilio, who rather than draw his sword
Chose exile here, ceased to be Meifod's lord.

It seems at first sight a fairly innocuous 'local' poem about the patron saint of a village church. Of course, it refers back to the Age of the Saints—the sixth century or thereabouts when Wales became a Christian country. It was a time constantly in Waldo's mind, and a matrix of his own crusade against 'Sovereignty' and war, because when monks like Gildas failed to persuade the warlords to mend their ways, they turned aside and founded instead their own alternative society devoted to peace. Tysilio was a lord of Powys in the sixth century who chose the monastic life.

He lived in Meifod in Maldwyn—the old Montgomeryshire, proverbial for its gentleness—but had to escape because some of his family tried to make him a prince.

That, then, is the Saint—Tysilio in an age of cruelty and greed given the light of Christ 'from beyond,' and joining in small companies to 'yoke the world one' into peace. Christ in Waldo Williams is chiefly the peacemaker of the Beatitudes, the teacher who spoke in the parables. Whether the poet believed that Christ saved him from his own personal sinfulness and damnation, and chose him to go to heaven—whether he was an orthodox Christian at all—is very doubtful. He certainly had mystical intimations of the coming of God's kingdom; but his most famous expression of these (in '*Mewn Dau Gae*') is rooted in ordinary people working together in the fields, not in any Christian Second Coming. Jesus, Tysilio, Mahatma Gandhi— people who are prepared to suffer in this world for the cause of brotherhood and peace—are those who have the light of Christ revealed to them. As he says in his poem about the raids on Swansea, thinking of his parents,

> In Christ's light is freedom had
> For any man that would be free.
> Blest, the day dawns that will hear them,
> Peacemakers, children of God.
> ('The Peacemakers')

But in fact the sonnet is not primarily about Tysilio. It is called 'Llandysilio-yn-Nyfed,' the parish, the village community gathered round Tysilio's church; and about Waldo himself as a boy as part of that community. It remembers the experience of waiting outside for the New Year, of the bells ringing and the family going indoors filled with wonder. Such ritual interruptions of the everyday are designed to release the imagination to make contact with what is important—in this case, the Light that manifested Christ to Tysilio. On a purely empirical level, that is what the poem is about. It is a picture of a community in action, at one of its moments of remembrance and hope, taking sustenance from the past to give to the future. It is this 'brotherhood,' that Waldo always opposes to 'Sovereignty' and temporal power. Like the early monks round Tysilio, it is a community 'without exploit of cities,' a small company that yet 'yokes the world one.'

But even that is not what the sonnet is really about. Its first sentence is not about the past, neither Tysilio's exile nor Waldo's own boyhood. It begins with the present: '*Mynych rwy'n syn*'—'Often I'm amazed.' What should give us a jolt is the fullstop. One is tempted to read it as simply, 'I am often amazed by the way light came from beyond to illumine Christ to Tysilio and his chosen ones,' and so on, making it just the pious amazement of a Church historian. But it isn't that. 'Often I am amazed.' As one reads the poem, one suddenly sees that there are three times involved, each with its own future implied. First (in inverse order of appearance) there is the time of Tysilio's choice of exile rather than the power of the sword, when the small companies of monks yoked the world one and salvation was like a clear flame. Secondly there is the poet's own boyhood, on New Year's eve, when the bells of the church rang in hope for a better year. And thirdly, there is now, the poet being amazed.

Read in this way, the lines about the light coming to reveal Christ to the elect ones when *our* life (*ein* byw—my italics) was greedy and cruel, without any great purpose or ideal—these lines need not simply refer to the collapse of values after the fall of Rome. After all, the Dark Ages were not the only time where life has been cruel, greedy and lacking in ideals. Like all Waldo's mature work his last poem refers ultimately to the struggle against Sovereignty and war-making now and in his own lifetime. The amazingness of the Light making clear the ways of Peace and the rescue of community and brotherhood in the teeth of war—that's what he wonders at, '*mynych*,' often—in fact, one could almost say, always. 'Llandysilio-yn-Nyfed' is as much a war-poem, in its own way, as '*Dan y Dyfroedd Claear*' ('Under the Gentle Waters)' after one of the great battles of the Pacific, or 'The Peacemakers'—

Rose-red sky above the snow
Where bombed Swansea is alight,
Full of my father and mother I go,
I walk home in the night.
They are blest beyond hearing,
Peacemakers, children of God . . .

What is their estate tonight,
Tonight, with the world ablaze?
Truth is with my father yet,
Mother with forgiveness stays.
The age will be blest that hears them,
Peacemakers, children of God.

THE GAME AND THE HORROR

'My great bow Gandiva', says Arjuna in the Bhagavad-Gita, 'falls from my hands, and the skin of my flesh is burning; I am no longer able to stand because my mind is whirling and wandering.' That moment of horror before the nightmare of fratricide is echoed in Waldo Williams's poems from the early forties. '*O Bridd*,' for instance, 'O soil of the earth,' is a wildly expressionistic piece where he sees the very soil we live on as evil and corrupt—

> Your red flowers are pox,
> Your yellow flowers pus.
> I'll not move. I've nowhere to go.
> Your fever has moved to my blood.
> I've seen the filthy maw
> Open and say, 'Ho, brother'—
> In the blood pit, my brother's
> Squeal sucked through his nape,
> Legs and no feet, my brother . . .
>
> She pushes us behind, our mother.
> She grimaces through the window.
> Shouts, 'Ho, people, providence!'
> She cackles over destruction.

The poem ends with a vision of God waiting in the Antarctic wastes: the only real value is in the absence of soil, the negation of life. Arjuna falls into despair because he is required to fight and kill the members of his actual family; but of course Waldo's despair is more universal because he believes *all* men are his brothers. '*O Bridd*' marks a fundamentally immature position where it is impossible to stay sane for very long. Waldo was rescued from it by his relationship with his wife Linda before her early death, and by his own faith in the goodness of things struggling to be good; but he kept '*O Bridd*' in his collection, presumably as a touchstone of the nightmare he and the world had suffered at that time.

It is surely with that nightmare that any war-poetry of our time must start, no matter how it is transcended, protested about or accepted. But, as I say, as a boy I appreciated the Second World War as a kind of game—one could almost call it a kind of intellectual soap-opera. Of course it did have emotional overtones. I was fortunate in that no one belonging to my family was killed or even wounded—apart from my Uncle Jack, who suffered multiple injuries in a traffic accident as a soldier in the Royal Army Ordnance Corps.* Nor do I remember any of our neighbours having close members of their family killed. So I was hardly in contact with the war as a bringer of grief. On the other hand, my parents were stranded in India and could not return: I did not see my father from 1937, when I was six, to 1945, when I was fourteen. My mother had come back briefly in 1939, so my memory of her was more recent. And of course there were other family disruptions as well. On the whole, though, this emotional aspect of the war was compartmentalised—*archived*, in computer jargon—and it was not finally faced or made available to my poetry until the late eighties when I wrote an elegy for my father in the fifth section of 'Castles.'

Nevertheless I always felt I knew about war—it was a constant background to my consciousness—although, apart from one very early and unsuccessful sonnet about our air-raid shelter, I never wrote about the Second World War as such. There are no lyrics about it in my collection; nor did it happen to come into any of my odes or gift-poems to specific individuals. On the other hand, in at least four of the longer and generally multiform poems that I call symphonies, war does figure as a subject. In the second ('The Bombing of Guernica') and the fifth ('Elegy for the Welsh Dead') it forms the main topic; while in the third ('Day Movements'), sixth ('Castles') and seventh ('All Hallows') it represents a major motif in the work, as it does also in my play *Branwen*.

---

* He used to supply me with empty bullets, mortar bombs and hand grenades, which we kept in a drawer in the kitchen, and even the odd bunch of cordite that looked like those incense sticks that hippies used to burn. It burnt brightly but did not explode unless it was detonated in a closed space. Presumably all this lovely armoury was classed as sub-standard rejects.

'The Bombing of Guernica' was part of the attempt, after the *Lizbook* and *Asymptotes*, to banish the subjunctive mood and the quasi-allegorical narrative from my work. My friend Bernard Rands the modernist composer suggested that we might collaborate in a cantata—not that he would have called it that!—for voices and instruments. He was at that time a Quaker, and very much preoccupied with pacifism. I had just read an account in a weekly magazine of the bombing of Guernica in the Spanish Civil War, which moved me, both as a human document and because it made me confront my own memories of watching Liverpool burn in the blitz. I knew of Picasso's painting, and that it had a bull in agony in it, but I had never yet seen it reproduced. It was not part of the poem's inspiration, save that in one place in the original version I mentioned a bull 'ranting at its tormentors' which was a nod in Picasso's direction—no more than that.

Could I fit my childish apprehension of war as a game into the horror I felt now at the idea of mass-murder and indiscriminate violence on the part of the state?

I read the magazine article in heraldic terms. The poem was built in five sections, in two-, three-, four-, five- and then again two-line stanzas respectively. For the first section I wanted static phrases, to suggest the still-life effect of early morning in the countryside, with Basque peasants getting up for work:

> Dark labourers pondered this April day
> the black enrobement of fat wives.
>
> Still life of an early morning. Harsh shadow and hard light.
> Tenderness and brutality in the gesture of laying a cup.
>
> Barn life. Yard life. Devotional
> chickens peck and squawk in the muck.

This is the norm of the poem—a mixture of brutality and tenderness that signals family life. I suppose the word 'pondered' suggests to me those early Picasso 'blue-period' paintings where the figures have a kind of brooding fragility, or, nearer home, the Bardsey fishermen in Brenda Chamberlain's pictures. The hens seem to have come in from our Hafod days of toy wars in the garden! Into this adagio the next section intrudes with *ad hoc* mythology:

> Old fury to old fury
> rumours with jeering malice
> what their own Swastika shall do.
>
> (Swastika, hope of the world,
> whose eyes bulge through thick spectacles
> to a yawning sun . . .)
>
> Hag unto hag reports
> this mourning that shall come to market
> like a farmer.

Swastika is the 'hero' of the poem, the embodiment of Nazi brutality, proclaimed as 'hope of the world' yet unable to see or feel properly and ultimately boring and destructive. The hags gather like converts to a new religion of malice. Guernica (as my note says) was bombed on a market-day, in order to increase the terror.

The third section moves out of the semi-darkness into the brightness of the sky, where the German aircraft (nicknamed 'the black birds' by the Spaniards) are moving into the attack:

> The black birds stand in the corners of the sky.
> Their talons are bright,
> their eyes dull with the mechanical
> violence of street louts.
>
> The black birds are ultimate cynics. Sunlight
> is pretext to be dead,
> to be herded into death like cattle,
> to kill with the brilliant gold of bullets.
>
> They lift their talons to the sky, these black birds,
> and delicately tilt their wings
> to a precision of narrow prey.
> They pockmark the cobbles with gold.

They are Swastika's servants, cynical, brutal. The flash of their bullets on the cobbles gave me 'gold' which from now on, as Ian Gregson remarks,* is part of the symbolism that organises the poem 'in advance' (I know what he means by this phrase, but it is not literally true: I just worked on the suggestion of the poem itself as I wrote it, in the way a musician develops the motifs implicit in a phrase). Gregson says that the colour symbolism contrasts yellow and black, but I see the contrast as threefold: black, gold and yellow. Black is the colour of the birds, of the 'enrobement' of the labourers' wives, of the charred face of the child. Gold is the colour of bullets, of raging fire, of bloodshed in the sunlight; somewhere in the background is the idea that all this is due to the workings of money. At the end 'the bones of vomiting gold' gathers up all these suggestions into a complex nightmare image. Yellow, finally, is the colour of nature—of the sky, of the rock out of which Guernica (the 'saffron city') is made—in this sun-soaked landscape contrasted with the blue of the Atlantic.

The central section of the poem, and the longest, describes the actual bombing of the town in a very mannerist style, using a complex of metaphor and symbolism to suggest and yet distance the hysteria and panic. Much of the language is playing with religious terminology, introduced by the bride at the churchdoor smiling at the 'golden suitor'—the bullet. Old women 'at solemn vespers of their toothless gossip' run to hide from pain's 'undiscriminating phallus of gold'—the bullets don't discriminate in their lust between bride and old hags. The priest carries Calvary—he is taking the sacrificial Host to the sick and dying, but also is himself carrying the cross in the way he dies spreadeagled on the road 'in the panic of a calling far beyond his'—that is, the calling of Swastika or the black birds, which is beyond the reach of the salvation that has called him and given him his priestly vocation.

The proud birds 'look uncomplainingly down at the saffron city.' As it were, they 'ponder' it, as the dark labourers pondered their wives. The gold blood (in an image which combines bride

---

* 'The Modernism of Anthony Conran' in *The Welsh Connection*, edited by W.S. Tydeman (Gomer, 1986)

and hag in one) is 'inviting as a widow.' One critic found this image too lightweight for the context; but within the stylistic framework of the poem it surely sums up the whole sadistic sexuality implicit from the start. Swastika's drum—the bombing—is like the Pied Piper's pipe, calling (again that word) rats from quaking holes.

The poem is very uneasily balanced—deliberately so—between the sense of a game, a linguistic game, a game with toy monsters; and, on the other side, the nightmare feeling of terror and protest and panic. As Ian Gregson very perceptively says,

> the poem's self-conscious aestheticism is actually used for non-aesthetic purposes: it refers to a state of mind which can regard the blitzing of Guernica like an author merely inventing it.

Gregson sees how the 'heraldry' is used for a political end—

> for it helps to characterise Fascism in the way it suggests a value system, ferociously hierarchical and pre-occupied with the aesthetics of violence.

It is when he applies this to the last section, however, that I begin to have doubts:

> In the fourth section,* future mornings are compared to authors or painters with their calculating selectivity:
>
> > Blossoming mornings of winter,
> > put no face to the child that sleeps.
> >
> > Put no feature, no eye or lip,
> > to the body that sleeps in frost.
> >
> > Don't remember the sickness of touching
> > that smouldering charred face

---

* Fifth, in the numbering used in this essay.

or the tomb we founded for God
on bones of vomiting gold.

Strict acid light of morning,
put no face to the child that sleeps.

Partly it is my feeling that mornings don't remember anyway—it is we who remember, not mornings, so in some complex sense the figure of speech is not quite a straight metaphor; and partly that I have always in my mind Lorca's '*Llanto por Ignacio Sánchez Mejías,*' the great lament for the bullfighter:

> *¡Que no quiero verla!*
>
> *Dile a la luna que venga,*
> *que no quiero ver la sangre*
> *de Ignacio sobre la arena.*
>
> *¡Que no quiero verla!*
>
> *La luna de par en par.*
> *Caballo de nubes quietas,*
> *y la plaza gris del sueño*
> *con sauces en las barreras.*
>
> *¡Que no quiero verla!*
>
> *Que mi recuerdo se quema.*
> *¡Avisad a los jasmines*
> *con su blancura pequeña!*
>
> *¡Que no quiero verla!*

I do not want to see it! Tell the moon to come, for I do not want to see Ignacio's blood on the sand. I do not want to see it! The moon wide open. Horse of still clouds, and the dream's grey bullring with willows in the barriers. I do not want to see it! For my remembrance burns. Warn the jasmines with their small whiteness! I do not want to see it!

(trans. J.L. Gili)

The last section of 'The Bombing of Guernica' has a closer relationship to Spanish poetry even than that, for it is a kind of nightmare parody of one of the most beautiful of Lope de Vega's lyrics:

> *Mañanicas floridas*
> *del frío invierno,*
> *recordad a mi niño*
> *que duerme al hielo.*
> *Mañanas dichosas*
> *del frío diciembre,*
> *aunque el cielo os siembre*
> *de flores y rosas,*
> *pues sois rigurosas*
> *Y Dios es tierno,*
> *recordad a mi niño*
> *que duerme al hielo.*

> Blossoming early mornings of cold winter, remember my child who is sleeping in the frost. Fortunate mornings of cold December, although the sky scatters flowers and roses on you, you being strict and God being tender, remember my child, who is sleeping in the frost.
>
> (trans. J.M. Cohen)

Lope de Vega is himself remembering with great tenderness the child who is dead, asleep in the frost. The beautiful early morning of winter is rigorous, but not cruel; and God is tender. The poet asks the morning though it so lovely with the colours, like flowers, that the sky scatters over it, not to forget the human child. In my poem, however, I do not want to see the dead child: his or her end was so horrific, it is better forgotten. The rigour of the winter morning has become a 'strict acid light' to dissolve away the nightmare of the charred face. God is dead, and we have made his tomb—and by implication the tomb of all tenderness—in those 'bones of vomiting gold.'

That is certainly how I meant the poem to be read; but I am not certain that Gregson's reading may not be equally valid. I look back on my childhood, with its over-riding sense of playing at war under the great shadow of my parents' absence, and it seems to me a bit crypto-fascistic. Perhaps in 'The Bombing of Guernica' my horror at the destruction of children does indeed verge on the 'calculating selectivity' Gregson talks about. Is there a break between the consciousness of the first four sections and that of the final lament? or is there not? If there is, then my memory of what I intended is correct; but if there is not, and the lament is an ironical exercise in wiping the slate clean with 'calculating selectivity,' then Gregson is right. I am not sure it actually matters to the poem as a whole, whichever way you read it. There is no doubt that the reader is intended to 'place' Swastika and his work as subhuman, whether this includes forgetting the victims or not; the horror and the pity will come through regardless.

*   *   *

As I say, 'The Bombing of Guernica,' attempted to reconcile the two sides of my apprehension of war—the heroic game and the nightmare horror—by selecting a scene where all our dislike is rightly focussed on the players of the game (Swastika and his black birds) and all our sympathy on the victims of the nightmare (the people and particularly the children of Guernica). I was able to present such a selective picture as a vision of modern war because modern war (in Dresden, in Hiroshima, frequently in Vietnam) is often itself selective in this way. But as a total vision of war, it clearly won't wash. It wasn't true even to my own limited experience.

War is something we make, something we do; not simply something we suffer. My third 'symphony', 'Day Movements,' in a couple of sections contrasts these two aspects of it, the doing and the suffering. 'Day Movements' was commissioned as a radio poem and I wrote it as a choreography or 'dance' for four voices. The pattern it makes in the listener's mind is more or less abstract, but the time scale involves a day's passage from dawn to morning to night and back to dawn again. The sections mostly involve a contrast between various kinds of sleep and various kinds of waking or realisation. Thus lovers, waking at dawn, prepare to part. The soul like St John of the Cross *'en una noch' oscura*'—one dark night'- with my 'love's anxieties flaming within me,' leaves its home in 'the better-class suburbs of death' and goes out into the darkness of God. Mary Magdelene walks like a 'somnambulist of grief' towards the grave where they have put her Lord. Jesus, the 'gardener of death,' dresses himself in the tomb before rolling aside the stone to wait for the first guest.

It is at this point, with Jesus the host waiting for his guests, that the two war sections occur. As Guernica had been full of Spanish poetry, so these are based on Welsh: the first on the 'Hirlas' poem usually attributed to Prince Owain Cyfeiliog of Powys. The prince and his warband have returned from a raid to release a prisoner somewhere on the English border, perhaps round Wrexham in Maelor. They are feasting after the battle and the poet tells his cupbearer to take round the 'long blue horn' full of mead to the various warriors who in turn are praised for their part in the battle. But when the cupbearer comes to Moreiddig, the others tell him that Moreiddig is dead, and the poetry turns briefly from exultation to lament. The 'Hirlas' poem begins,

> There was a shout as dawn was breaking -
> Enemies sending us noisy bad-fortune.
> Our men red-speared, after the wearisome
> March to the township wall of Maelor ...

Here is my adaptation of it:

> Sure enough, just as dawn broke, the bastards
> Started to yell blue murder.
> We didn't half bless 'em.
> We were dead tired, what with carrying rifles
> All that rough country to Maelor.
> Just the same, I put 'em straight in.
> If you provoke a shindy
> It's yr own look-out
> If it does you no good.
>
> What about you, Cynfelin?
> Go on, give him a drink.
> God, he looks tanked up with it already!

> Now, now, more respect for a soldier
> If you value your skin. Give him his due.
> And how about Griffith—where's his glass?
>
> What's yr name, oy, you with the bottle,
> Give some of this to Rhys, my old friend Rhys.
> What d'ye mean, didn't I pay for it, boys,
> And isn't it damn good stuff?
> Cocky it makes you feel
> And a bit sad too—
> Gets the old hormones busy.
>
> Friend, take that Morgan there an extra dose.
> He's earned it, way he worked this morning.
>
> Oh it's not Morgan . . . Dead, did you say.
> Well, well. That's a sod isn't it?
> Always good for a song was Morgan
> And a brave man too . . .
>
> Well, we had them on the hop, and caught the boss
> With a mint of money on him, why I don't know.
> We were reeking of sweat, coming back
> Down the valley with the sun right on us . . .

The piece is no more than a dramatic sketch—certainly not a full-blown heroic panegyric. It does show, though, an awareness of the decency of soldiers—actually a civilized and learnt thing. It is also set in Wales. If the Germans had invaded Britain, it could have been like this; but in the sixties, when it was written, there were Welshmen considering taking to arms, I.R.A. fashion, to save their country from English infiltration and power. Had this happened on any scale I do not know what my reaction (or that of many of my friends) would have been. Would I, for instance, have handed over a Welsh guerilla-fighter to the police?

Following war as something we do, then, war as something we suffer. The next piece in 'Day Movements' is a lament by a woman for her lover. Perhaps it is Morgan's young widow who imagines him dead on the hillside. Again, I was imitating—though this time a good deal more vaguely—a Welsh model: the ninth-century 'ballad' or saga-*englynion* of the Cynddylan cycle, in which the girl Heledd laments Cynddylan's death at the hands of the English invaders of Powys. Here for instance is part of the *englynion*, which describe the white-tailed or sea-eagles from the river Eli now the Meheli—feasting on the dead:

> Eagle of Eli, loud was its cry tonight—
> Had drunk of a pool of blood,
> The heart's blood of Cynddylan Wyn.
>
> Eagle of Eli, it cried out tonight,
> It swam in men's blood.
> There in the trees! And I've misery on me . . .
>
> Eagle of Eli that watches the seas,
> In the estuaries fishes no longer.
> In the blood of men it calls its feast.

And the eagle of Pengwern answers it—

> Grey-capped eagle of Pengwern, tonight
> Is its claw aloft,
> Greedy for the flesh I love.

We no longer have sea-eagles in Wales, but crows and ravens would certainly serve the same purpose as scavengers. Here is the lament I wrote:

> I shall never wake up to see him.
> I shall never sense his breathing beside me.
> His sleep will not touch my breasts.
>
> I shall never be early to bed with him
> Or casual at breakfast.
> There's no tempting him to love me.
>
> Sheep take the grass of the cwm.
> They flow like a shadow, like a scattered cloud
>   over the grass.
> The sheep are avoiding him, lying there, this minute.

What's the red darkness on the ground?
Shy away from it, follow-my-leader
This way and that.

Down the grey corridors of rock and sky
Strutting in the wind and circling
The ravens, the ravens, they have entered, they caress his
    body.

They know my darling is dead,
As only I know it otherwise—
Because it is food.

The bitterness of his stretching
On the grey hill
Under my thoughts,
Under the red raven's claw . . .

*   *   *

That is the background, subjectively speaking, to the fifth of my symphonies, *Elegy for the Welsh Dead, killed in the Falkland Islands, 1982*. Like the other war-pieces, it uses earlier and non-English poetry as a model: in this case Aneirin's *Gododdin*, a series of heroic elegies commemorating the heroes of a warband that went from Dun Eiddyn (Edinburgh) to try and re-take Catraeth (Catterick in Yorkshire) from the invading English, under the leadership of Mynyddog Mwynfawr, the chief of the Otadini, a British tribe called Y Gododdin in Welsh. He feasted and trained his warriors for a year in preparation, but though they fought bravely all but a few were killed and mourned in this ancient poem or poetic sequence by Aneirin. Traditionally, the *Gododdin* is attributed to the sixth century; though it is in the language we know as Welsh or Cymraeg, it is a British poem, not a Welsh one.

I was in Ireland when the Falklands affair started, and from that distance it seemed unbelievably foolish. The Thatcher government had obviously made a cock-up of the situation, trying to wriggle out of a colonial commitment that no longer made much sense to Whitehall, without losing face. As with the Gulf

War later on, a footling dictator had been encouraged to chance his arm by the contradictory signals coming from the big powers. Thatcher was unpopular, however; and she obviously decided to do a Winston Churchill, with the wretched Falklands (or Malvinas as they were called in Spanish—Ynysoedd Malfinas in Welsh) as her beaches of Dunkirk and Battle of Britain rolled into one.

For a short time everyone was huffing and puffing, and peace was possible. Then (I was still in Ireland) the great expeditionary force was kitted out and sent on its way. I was still incredulous about the whole thing, particularly because I realised that war was now inevitable: once you send an army you cannot unsend it without seeming indecisive. From being a negotiating position, with each side offering face-saving concessions, it becomes a matter of making 'the enemy' retract to the utmost. You ignore any concessions which try to save face for the other side, because what the situation now demands is not peace but victory. In fact, as with Iraq and the United States, the logic of the game makes negotiation itself a bluff in a military strategy. Of course, you have respectable precedents for your logic, if Britain and France had not appeased Nazi Germany, it is possible that the Second World War need never have been fought. A feature of such situations, therefore, is always an implied or explicit comparison of your enemy with Hitler; and since dictators often do have a lot in common with each other, propaganda has a field day.

When I came back to Wales I was astonished and dismayed by the war fever everywhere. It was a re-cap of my boyhood, as it were, except that I myself was very different. I knew enough about war, though, to suspect that the expeditionary force was based on very precarious foundations. Air power is essential in such affairs, and as far as one could tell, our aircraft carrier capacity was quite small. Two or three well-aimed torpedoes or missiles (their modern equivalents) would probably have scotched our chances for good. But tinpot dictators are often useless militarily. The Argentines proved no better at deploying their considerable strength than Saddam Hussein later. When they did move, they used the wrong pieces, with an eye to prestige and propaganda effect rather than military advantage. The ancient cruiser *Belgrano* would have been as useful against a modern fleet as a javelin against a machine-gun.

Wales was, however, not quite so caught up in jingoism and war communiques that didn't tell you anything, as England seemed to be. Pacifists were holding crowded meetings in Bangor and Caernarfon. Plaid Cymru was about the only party to come out solidly against the war.

It was then that I heard that forty-three Welsh soldiers had been killed when an Argentine air-born missile damaged a British ship offshore. In the Welsh weekly newspaper, *Y Cymro* there was a preliminary list of nine soldiers who had died in the incident, as follows:

>Peter Edwards near Denbigh
>Malcolm Wigley of Connah's Quay
>Russell Carlisle of Rhuthun
>Clifford Elley of Pontypridd
>Philip Sweet of Cwmbach
>Nigel Rowberry of Cardiff
>Anthony Jones of Carmarthen
>Ian Dale of Pontypridd
>Colin Parsons of Cardiff

I was certainly in a very emotional state—angry, grieving and excitable. I started to write a series of elegies for the dead, based on the *Gododdin*, fully intending (when I had the complete list) to mention each of the forty-three by name. For the moment I had only nine names, however; and I did not want to begin with Peter Edwards because the *Cymro* had an article about him and I didn't at this stage want extraneous human interest. The whole point of naming the dead would have been compromised if they had been other than complete strangers to me or to the reader. After two introductory stanzas comparing the expedition that tried to retake Catraeth with Mrs Thatcher's expedition to retake the Falklands (or Malvinas) from the Argentine invaders, I started to go down the list, beginning with Malcolm Wigley of Connah's Quay. When I came to Nigel Rowberry of Cardiff, I thought, O dear, another English name—surely I cannot have all English names! So I skipped him for the moment and went on with Tony Jones of

Carmarthen. Unfortunately, though I'd wanted to write a section on each of the soldiers, the poem ground to a halt. I would certainly have gone on with Nigel Rowberry if it had been possible. I had no prejudice against Cardiff or the other big towns. (In the full list of casualties, five came from Cardiff, two from Newport, none from Swansea or Merthyr.) Ian Dale and Colin Parsons would have been more problematic, because the article, once again, gave specific facts about them. I also very much regret overlooking the woman civilian who died with the soldiers.

It seemed to me that it was no part of my job as a poet to 'humanise' these men. As Ian Gregson has pointed out, the more literary I could be the better, because that would leave the names space to be themselves. My purpose was simply to weave a decorative and serious pattern to express my grief and anger, and to put the soldiers in a context both of heroic tradition and what seemed to me the political hypocrisy that sent them to their deaths.

ELEGY FOR THE WELSH DEAD, IN THE FALKLAND ISLANDS, 1982

Gwŷr a aeth Gatraeth oedd ffraeth eu llu.
Glasfedd eu hancwyn, a gwenwyn fu.
       Y Gododdin (6th century)

(Men went to Catraeth, keen was their company.
They were fed on brown mead, and it proved poison.)

Men went to Catraeth. The luxury liner
For three weeks feasted them.
They remembered easy ovations,
Our boys, splendid in courage.
For three weeks the albatross roads,
Passwords of dolphin and petrel,
Practised their obedience.
Where the killer whales gathered,
Where the monotonous seas yelped.
Though they went to church with their standards
Raw death has them garnished.

Men went to Catraeth. The Malvinas
Of their destiny greeted them strangely.
Instead of affection there was coldness,
Splintering iron and the icy sea,
Mud and the wind's malevolent satire.
They stood nonplussed in the bomb's indictment.

Malcolm Wigley of Connah's Quay. Did his helm
Ride high in the war-line?
Did he drink enough mead for that journey?
The desolated shores of Tegeingl,
Did they pig this steel that destroyed him?
The Dee runs silent beside empty foundries.
The way of the wind and the rain is adamant.

Clifford Elley of Pontypridd. Doubtless he feasted.
He went to Catraeth with a bold heart.
He was used to valleys. The shadow held him.
The staff and the fasces of tribunes betrayed him.
With the oil of our virtue we have annointed
His head, in the presence of foes.

Phillip Sweet of Cwmbach. Was he shy before girls?
He exposes himself now to the hags, the glance
Of the loose-fleshed whores, the deaths
That congregate like gulls on garbage.
His sword flashed in the wastes of nightmare.

Russell Carlisle of Rhuthun. Men of the North
Mourn Rheged's son in the castellated vale.
His nodding charger neighed for the battle.
Uplifted hooves pawed at the lightning.
Now he lies down. Under the air he is dead.

Men went to Catraeth. Of the forty-three
Certainly Tony Jones of Carmarthen was brave.
What did it matter, steel in the heart?
Shrapnel is faithful now. His shroud is frost.

With the dawn men went. Those forty-three,
Gentlemen all, from the streets and byways of Wales,

> Dragons of Aberdare, Denbigh and Neath—
> Figment of empire, whore's honour, held them.
> Forty-three at Catraeth died for our dregs.

The lines I quote from *Y Gododdin* do not imply they were drunk going into battle or poisoned by bad liquor. 'To pay for your mead' for a warrior was to fight bravely in return for your keep &c. These warriors fought bravely but died—the mead they drank led to their deaths.

Y Gododdin names many of the warriors and describes how brave they were. Many stanzas begin 'Men went to Catraeth.' There are many other cross-references to the ancient elegies in my poem. I have several times been asked to annotate these and other semi-quotations; this is perhaps a good place to do it.

In the first paragraph, then, the feasting of the warband at Dun Eiddyn is remembered in the luxury liner that took the soldiers to war. 'Our boys' was how Mrs Thatcher used to refer to them. 'Though they went to church etc.' misquotes the lines in *Y Gododdin*:

> Although they might go to shrines to do penance,
> This much was certain, death would transfix them.

In the third paragraph, Connah's Quay—in what was Flintshire, now Clwyd, the ancient Tegeingl (accented on the first syllable) or country of the Deceangli, a British tribe—was opposite the great Deeside steelworks, now closed, which gave employment to the whole area. You don't strictly 'pig' steel as far as I know—the term is used of an oblong mass of iron ('pig-iron') from a smelting furnace—the verb is rare but still used and too good to lose! 'The way of the wind and the rain was adamant' to an English reader recalls the song in *Twelfth Night* about the nature of man:

> When that I was but a tiny little boy,
>   With a heigh-ho, the wind and the rain etc.

(and therefore makes a pun on Adam-ant) or perhaps more

vaguely *King Lear* in the storm; but to a Welsh reader it is a quotation from the elegy on the last Prince of independent Wales, Llywelyn ap Gruffydd, killed by Edward I in 1282. The poet at the climax of his lament cries out that the world is destroyed:

> See you not the way of the wind and the rain? . . .
> See you not the sun hurtling through the sky,
> And that the stars are fallen? &c.

Now 'Clifford Elley of Pontypridd'—Pontypridd is in the south Wales mining valleys, hence 'he was used to valleys' and the pun on the twenty-third psalm:

> Yea, though I walk through the valley of the shadow of death, yet I will fear no evil; thy rod and thy staff comfort me. Thou hast prepared a table before me in the presence of my enemies. Thou annointest my head with oil.

A 'fasces' was a bundle of rods with an axe in the middle carried before a high magistrate in Rome. (The word 'fascist' comes from Mussolini's megalomaniac use of it as a badge to signify that his party would restore Roman glory to Italy: a fact not without relevance to my poem.) A tribune was an officer who represented the Roman plebs, as opposed to the patrician consul. Therefore, by analogy, a member of the House of Commons who represented us.

'Was he shy before girls?' like the warrior in *Y Gododdin* who was 'breathless before a girl, yet fierce in battle.' It is very important that I knew nothing about Phillip Sweet of Cwmbach. Even so I was uneasy of giving offence, and when I first published these lines I tried to disguise his identity.

'Russell Carlisle of Rhuthun'—Rhuthun (or Ruthin) is a town in modern Clwyd or north-east Wales. The whole valley between the Clwydian hills and the Denbighshire uplands is littered with castles—the one at Ruthin has been converted into a hotel. The name Carlisle, however, is from a town in the north-west of England, once part of the ancient British kingdom of Rheged, what the Welsh call the Old North. So in both senses the soldier was 'a man of the North', mourned by his compatriots.

'Uplifted hooves pawed at the lightning'—see the *Book of Job*, the description of the war-horse in Chapter 39, verses 19-25. Too long to quote and not a precise reference, but I had it in mind.

'With the dawn men went'—a quotation from *Y Gododdin*, used to introduce a number of stanzas.

'Gentlemen all'—undoubtedly I owe the word 'gentlemen' to the last section of David Jones's *In Parenthesis*, where the Queen of the Woods distributes her gifts to the dead soldiers:

> She speaks to them according to precedence. She knows what's due to this elect society. She can choose twelve gentle-men.

I call the Welsh soldiers dragons, partly because the flag of Cadwaladr, the legendary last king of Britain before the English conquest, was the Red Dragon. This was used by the Welshman Henry Tudor as his flag when he conquered England to become Henry VII. It then became the Welsh flag, so a 'dragon' is a 'kenning' or poetic nickname for a Welshman. But 'dragon' was also used by the Welsh poets to signify a great warrior, as in the elegy on Llywelyn ap Gruffydd already mentioned.

* * *

John Barnie in his essay 'Heroic Laughter,' (which I've already mentioned) thinks I'm devaluing heroism in this poem. He takes me to task for using the *Gododdin* lines as an epigraph, because, quoted out of context, the emphasis is on 'poison':

> The implication is that the year's feasting before that battle was a poison-cup, and Anthony Conran parallels, rather than contrasts, this with the guardsmen who 'feasted' for three weeks in a luxury liner on the way to their death.
>
> Placed in context, however, the lines from Y Gododdin have a different significance. The warriors may have drunk a bitter drink, but they died heroically, and the poem is a celebration of this as well as an elegy. As in Y Gododdin, Anthony Conran names the men who died:

> Certainly Tony Jones of Carmarthen was brave.
> What did it matter, steel in the heart?
> Shrapnel is faithful now. His shroud is frost.

The second line is ambiguous. It could mean 'steel in the heart did not matter, because he was brave.' A more likely meaning in the general context of the poem, however, is: 'what does bravery count for, when all it leads to is an early death?'

The answer of the heroic poet would be that if Tony Jones was brave at his death it did matter. It is possible to take Anthony Conran's position partly because we know, or suspect, that these guardsmen were not trained in, and never thought of themselves as operating within, a heroic code. Were the heroes of Catraeth watching pornographic videos when they died?

To take the last point first. If they were watching pornographic videos when they were killed, does it therefore follow that their claim to be mourned as heroes is invalidated? I didn't know they were when I wrote the poem, nor do I know now: but whether they were or not, does it affect their status as heroes? For all we know Achilles might have been committing buggery in his tent; he was certainly sulking. Heroes don't have to be morally perfect, just brave. And courage is an absolute, whether you approve of the aim of it or not. (It is typical of our fear of words that we're horrified when someone calls a terrorist 'brave.' Of course a terrorist can be brave and of course our acknowledgement of that fact does not mean we support terrorism. The tragedy of hell is not that it is evil, but that so much of it is good.)

As far as I can see, I stress the heroic quality of the guardsmen throughout the poem. Clifford Elley, for instance, 'went to Catraeth with a bold heart.' Phillip Sweet's sword 'flashed in the wastes of nightmare.' Russell Carlisle rode a horse that 'neighed for the battle.' The forty-three are 'gentlemen all.' They are 'dragons.' And if it be objected that such language is high-flown and metaphorical, and therefore suspect, I would agree that certain things undercut it and make it ironic, to a degree. To flash your sword in the wastes of nightmare is a complex image, more to do with imagination than actual deeds; but even so, it does not call in question the man's courage.

'Certainly Tony Jones of Carmarthen was brave' in modern usage expects the qualification 'but . . .' It seems to lead straight into Barnie's interpretation. However, it is the second time such an expression has occurred, and each time without a 'but' clause after it. I say of Clifford Elley,

> Doubtless he feasted.
> He went to Catraeth with a bold heart.

The syntax seems to me on a par with the rhetorical questions throughout: 'Did he drink enough mead for that journey?' Almost, the lines suggest older meanings, 'he feasted without doubt,' that is, not doubting his purpose; or 'truly Tony Jones was brave, there's no question of it.' The ambiguity is therefore not just in that one phrase, 'What did it matter?' but is everywhere insisted on. The syntax is deliberately odd—Wynn Thomas compares the effect to that of a translation. To say that 'steel in the heart' *has* to be taken as a metaphor for courage—what did bravery matter?—is immediately contradicted by the very next word: 'Shrapnel'—that is, bits of steel from the exploding missile—'is faithful now.' What did it matter?

To use Northrop Frye's useful taxonomy, the poem is ironic not low mimetic in mode: that is, it deals not with free agents on a par with ourselves but with heroes who are unfree, in bondage or in some way disabled from freedom. That is one reason why it was important not to have 'human interest' about any of the dead, because 'human interest' in the media assumes equality with ourselves, i.e. it is low mimetic. In the ironic mode (say, of *In Parenthesis*) the tragic is stripped of particularity: there is no reason why this man should die and not that—

> That swine Lillywhite has daisies to his chain—you'd hardly credit it.

The Queen of the Woods gives her prize of princely death without acknowledging life's 'impudent equality.'

'Elegy for the Welsh Dead' has elements of the surreal. It is close to dream imagery—particularly in the opening paragraphs where the journey on the luxury liner is seen in about four different contexts at once; including that of coming home on board ship and finding it not home at all—'Instead of affection there was coldness'—but a court of law with violence as prosecuting counsel—'They stood nonplussed in the bomb's indictment.' [In Welsh circles at this time there was a constantly recurring 'folktale' of the Welsh soldier dying in battle suddenly finding that his adversary spoke Welsh, because he came from the Welsh colony, the Wladfa, in Patagonia; or sometimes it was the Argentine soldier who was dying, picked up by a Welshman and speaking Welsh in his agony. A further twist was when the Welshman recognised it as Welsh though he himself was a monoglot English-speaker.]

The hero creates meaning in his community by his death. That is his social function. My poem, insofar as it is explicit about these things and not simply a cri de coeur, is about the failure somewhere along the line of that process, so that heroic death is itself short-circuited. Men go to Catraeth, and what happens? They die to plug a gaping hole in British foreign policy.

> The two terms are:
> 1. What did it matter, Tony Jones being brave? He still died of shrapnel. The Wilfred-Owen bit.
> 2. What did it matter that he died of shrapnel, his heroic bravery was still a value. Shrapnel keeps faith with his courage. Frost is his shroud—'Rolled round in earth's diurnal course' and all that.

Both terms are really present all through the poem. The forty-three are dragons—heroes. Equally their lives are wasted.

I would want to claim heroic status for my poem. That is part of its surrealism. I am not, and never have been, simply re-hashing Wilfred Owen's pity-of-war-ism; though that too is part of the feeling, as John Barnie points out it must be. But the naming of heroes is what I'm on about, as much as the identification of victims.

John Barnie's essay centres on a discussion of the crucifixion as both heroic and non-heroic at once. *Eloi, eloi, lama sabachthani*—my God, my God, why have you forsaken me?—the non-heroic futility and lack of meaning; but also the heroic acceptance and realisation of his destiny—'It is finished,' or 'achieved.' In our time, the tension between the two has become surreal; but is it not also the stuff out of which tragedy is made? As a critic Barnie separates the two moments as opposites. In experience, they are really one thing. The hero as suffering servant—the hero as a nonsense. The hero as himself a critique of the heroic. Not that all this tragic hinterland is in my poem. But some of it is, surely. It is not just an expression of anger (though that's there all right) or pity for the young being betrayed.

WESTERN AND COUNTRY

John Barnie says that we no longer have an adequate language to describe heroic behaviour. But in the popular arts the hero is still portrayed—Barnie refers disdainfully to the end-line of a B-Western or gangster film, the 'shadow-play of the heroic tradition.' Surely this is just snobbery: the end of 'High Noon,' for instance, for all its sentiment, seems to me a very real heroic experience. The opening up of the American West was a heroic age, a period of cataclysmic social change, a folk-wandering comparable to the break-up of the Minoan or the Roman civilizations or the Viking explosion after the premature expansion of Charlemagne's empire. The ideology of the cowboy was heroic, but also sentimental: if we compare native American ballads—white American, that is—with the heroic ballads of the English-Gaelic frontier in Aberdeenshire, we notice a stiffness, a kind of blinkering by sentiment, that the Scots rarely have. The singer sits bolt upright, without expressionist gestures; but the tunes he sings to, the ancestors of Country and Western, are often quite soft, sentimental ditties, without any of the driving force of 'Earl Brand' or 'Johnnie Cock.' The Cowboy bard is not allowed by his puritan tradition to go into details of sexual behaviour that Scots ballad singers would treat as facts of life: not just incest but adultery is hidden behind the veil of sentiment. Cowboy songs are often first-person affairs, as Aberdeenshire ballads rarely are: they focus on the subject's feelings rather than the objective story-line. Also, the class-structure they emanate from is democratic: the hero, the villain, the gangster, are not aristocrats. They are ordinary folk caught up in circumstances for which their education and culture give them very little guidance or power to sublimate in aesthetic terms. But to deny the cowboy and the rustler heroic status seems just snobbery to me. The Western film-maker is on the whole very true to his tradition. 'High Noon' is the sort of epic structure one might have expected from the cowboy ballads. Like all epics, it describes a heroic world that has long disappeared but has left an enduring vision—even a source of education—behind it.

The white American ballad is undoubtedly one source of contemporary sensibility; but it has been masked to a large extent by its black shadow, the Blues. The Blues is everything the white Ballad is not. Though there are black heroic ballads, (that of John Henry the 'steel-driving man' for example) the black singer generally prefers the unheroic, the sufferer from social or sexual injustice, or alternatively the sinner saved by Jesus who can escape from such injustice through religion: the blues and the spiritual. Black singers are relaxed and often move about as they sing, their accompaniment is fluid and expressionist, even the words lack the kind of rigid order that a white ballad-singer aims for. They often give the impression that they are creating their music as they go along, which white singers hardly ever do. John Barnie tells us how much the blues mean to him, and I suspect that the culture of the English-speaking intelligentsia is largely blues-centred, though often at several removes from the real thing.

For some reason I cannot quite fathom, I find American folk culture, both white and black, more opaque and alien than almost any other. I can relatively easily respond to Nigerian drumming, Algerian oud-playing, even (which is quite hard) the hardanger fiddling of Western Norway; but Jazz and Blues and Blue-Grass I have to learn the hard way, even though I share a common language with it. It takes a long time before it does not all sound the same to me—which is, I take it, the break-through point in music as in language-acquisition. I suspect it is because I don't often encounter good jazz or good blues or blue-grass in the flesh; whereas I have met and listened to quite a few hardanger fiddlers!

What this means is that I cannot easily articulate my poetry either like a B-western or a gangster. I don't have that vein of sensibility—ultimately of the white ballad or 'the blues—easily available to me. Of course I look at such things now and then, and get caught up in the excitement of the chase. But it is quite rarely that I understand what's going on. My family have to explain to me afterwards; it is only then that I start taking it in.

On the other hand, once this education has been gone through, I do enjoy blues and jazz and even gangster films. I listen to my few jazz and blues records quite often in fact, though I rarely feel called upon to extend my range in that direction, and if I did, I don't think I'd know what to buy. Typically, I only started to appreciate such things as Bob Dylan (and even the Beatles) in 1969, after I'd seen the film 'Easy Rider.'

Obviously, the nearer American music is to European, the easier I find it—though there's a danger that I will respond to it as second-rate English or Irish or what not, rather than something good in itself. But for instance, I can relish the traditional ballad-singing of Sara Cleveland from up-state New York easier than Almeda Riddle from the Ozarks or Woodie Guthrie from Oklahoma. This is not, I'd emphasise, a value judgement. I value Almeda Riddle as highly as any English-language traditional singer anywhere; and Woodie Guthrie shows the wholesome creativity of white folksong in America, and goes far to explain why it has had such a commanding influence (through Country and Western and 'Folk') on worldwide popular music from Tipperary to New Guinea. It is simply a matter of ease of access. It means, for instance, that American Rock is largely an unknown continent to me. I'm still talking in terms of the sixties, and even then I can see the splendour of Jimmy Hendrix as one can see the hills of Cumbria from Snowdon; but I've never been there in the sense that I'd distinguish one Hendrix song from another or remember any of them individually as I do Bob Dylan's 'Desolation Row' or the Stones' 'Satisfaction.'

This American illiterateness has had severe consequences for my poetry. I did once try and write a twelve-bar blues, just to show willing, but every American friend I've shown it to has hated it on sight. The problem has something to do with dialect, I think, but mainly that I am treating as a kind of charade something which is flesh of their flesh, bone of their bone:

LAST TRAIN BLUES

Old puffing caterpillar mumbling on a leaf,
Hundred mile long is one hell of a leaf.
    Hundred mile long the tale of my grief.

My heart playing hooky as the train came in,
Sentry on a night off as the slowcoach train came in.
　　Man, have you heard of the wages of sin?

Never saw the hangman in the twelve-twenty's tail,
Sitting sly and nasty in the black rattling tail,
　　To put a noose round me, drag me down the rail.

It does sound lamentably Old World, doesn't it? Yet why isn't the form—as clear and definite a formal structure as any in Provençal poetry—usable for me? After all, if pushed, I could write a *canso* that didn't sound like dressing-up; and certainly a Petrarchan sonnet. Why not a blues?

FAIRY TALES

I had never been particularly interested in writing prose fiction. For one thing I could never think of plots; and for another the precise notation of experience—even imaginary experience—on its own terms has never meant much to me as a creative artist. Indeed I think of myself as a poet, not as a writer. However, when my daughters were small, I started to tell them bedtime stories, some of which became very elaborate, particularly the cycle of tales concerning a flute-player called Jonathan. I would start off,

> 'Once upon a time, Jonathan was . . .'

and we were away. I usually had not the faintest idea what the story would be about before I went into the bedroom, though sometimes stories were told several times, usually in answer to requests.

These were oral stories, therefore; and they compare in some respects with folktales. They are more like Grimm than they're like Hans Anderson. Whereas the story-writer's imagination is conditioned by feeling, the story-teller's is activated by intelligence. Compare the Hans Anderson's 'Little Mermaid' (a written story) with a genuine folktale from oral tradition like 'Snow White' in Grimm. Hans Anderson is interested in the emotional mileage he can get out of the mermaid's longing to be human. How she achieves humanity is painful and has no real relation to her situation. But the oral story-teller of 'Snow White' starts with an intellectual problem, the queen talking to her mirror:

> 'Mirror, mirror, on the wall,
> Who is the fairest of us all?'

The story-teller has no particular interest in the queen's jealousy which he takes for granted. The attention is fixed on how this jealousy can be evaded. Sometimes feelings provide the answer—

the huntsman has a soft heart, the dwarfs befriend Snow White, the prince falls in love with her. But often they do not, and cunning or common-sense have to be used—'Don't talk to old women trying to sell you apples!' In any case, the feelings are never the point of the story and are often fairly commonplace: princes, after all, can be expected to fall in love with damsels in distress.

The oral folktale is probably the most intellectual form in all literature: not in the sense that it deals with scientific or philosophical matters—though it is well equipped to do so—but simply that it is driven by the intellect, not primarily by the emotions. Several reasons can be given for this, such as the origin of the folktale in a society that has not yet come to emotional self-consciousness; or the fact that the story-tellers are often of the skilled artisan class, which is far and away the class most dependent on pure intelligence—anyone who doubts this should try building a house! One is reminded that Jesus, the teller of parables, was a carpenter by trade. But though such factors probably helped to make the oral tale popular, its intellectuality must always depend mainly on the fact of telling it, not writing it down. You are faced with an audience who want to know what happens next; and you have no time to concentrate on anything else except the intellectual puzzle of how to finish the plot in a satisfactory way. More than in any other fiction, the oral tale's plot is its *raison d'être*. The shaping of the plot is where the artistry of the teller lies. 'Elegant' solutions have to be found, as in mathematics, or the tale loses its point.

Of course, where the teller is sure of where he's going he can sometimes elaborate on the feelings involved. It is a kind of holiday from his main work, which is intelligence-driven. Particularly is this the case where humour or pathos are involved, because these are feelings which draw the audience into his story. But very often what looks like emotional elaboration is in fact formulaic, as in the 'runs' (verbally complex passages learnt off by heart and recited very quickly) of Irish folktale. The formulae look exasperatingly repetitious on the page, but in performance are enjoyed for their own sake. An example of this in my stories would be the sequences based on 'He looked up' in 'The Giant who didn't know how':

> Jonathan looked out of his cottage window and he saw, in the middle of the road, two enormous boots. He looked up, and he saw two legs in trousers above the boots. He looked up, and he saw a great leather belt above the legs. He looked up, and he saw an open-necked shirt above the belt. He looked up, and there on the top of the shirt was a huge pink head with a sandy-coloured beard on it.

This was the first story that I noted down immediately after I had told it and it remains an almost entirely oral tale, very close on the page to what it was when I told it.

Besides the intellectual basis of oral story-telling and the use of 'runs,' the told tale tends to differ in its construction from the written one. 'The Little Mermaid' starts at the beginning and goes on in roughly the same narrative mode until it gets to the end. That is, the narrative is linear. The end of the story is widely different from the beginning, but you go from A to B in more or less a straight line. It is true that certain scenes stand out: such as when the mermaid rescues the prince from drowning, or when she learns the cost of becoming human. But they do so because of their emotional poignancy, not because of the inter-personal drama they embody. And these 'special' scenes do not occur with any sort of regularity or pattern. Contrast 'Snow White,' where the story proceeds by a series of inter-personal dramas—evil queen and mirror, queen and hunter, hunter and Snow White, Snow White and the dwarfs, and so on. The purely narrative sections merely link the dramatic scenes with necessary information. What is more, these inter-personal dramas often make a formal pattern of their own: the queen's repeated questioning of the mirror has all the imaginative effect of a refrain. If the scenes are plotted, like with like, contrast with contrast, the told tale's patterning often emerges as three-dimensional rather than linear, with the end of the tale returning in some changed way to its beginning. Thus the action of 'Snow White' begins with the marriage of the evil queen in a royal court.

The hunter's evasion of the queen's command to murder Snow White takes the latter outside the court into the wilderness of forest and mountain. We then alternate between the two locations, court and wilderness, for the queen's own threefold attempt to kill her innocent rival—tightening her stays till she can't breathe, combing her hair with a magic comb, and selling her a poisoned apple. Finally it returns to the court—a different court but clearly of comparable status—for Snow White's own marriage and the overthrow and punishment of the wicked queen. Oral story-telling, in its three-dimensional structure, is closer to drama than it is to written fiction. That is why pantomime, the last traditional form of drama that is living and still productive, takes off from folktale and not usually from Hans Anderson.

These features of oral folktale are certainly present in my stories. On the whole they are organised in a series of interpersonal dramatic scenes. Often these scenes are in threes; and the climax is usually a return to the beginning but with changed conditions. 'The Magic Hollow,' for example, actually contains an unusual amount of narrative. Nevertheless, it is based on one act repeated three times. Jonathan and the King of the Underworld both go into the hollow and are made smaller; but finally the King of the Underworld goes into it, stays the same size and so destroys the evil magic. But equally important are the interpersonal scenes, where the King of the Underworld questions Jonathan, where Jonathan questions the King of the Underworld, and where the King of the Underworld questions the fairy folk and seeks their aid.

The patterning is quite often elaborate: ABC motifs at the beginning of a tale might be echoed by the same motifs at the end but in reverse order, CBA. As with the intellectuality of the oral tale, so its three-dimensional patterning seems to stem from its very nature. It arises out of an I-you situation, as drama does. The teller physically confronts his audience in three-dimensional space. What he creates is a pattern of words that his audience hear—out there, so to speak. His story is like a yo-yo, leaving the charmed circle at the beginning only to return to it at the end. This is not a conscious thing, or only secondarily so. As the teller becomes more confident in his art, naturally he becomes more conscious of his technique and more able to use it for particular purposes such as humour, parody or pathos.

Another feature these stories have in common with folktales is the comparative bareness of their openings. For a writer, the opening paragraphs of his story are crucial. He spends a great deal of effort interesting the reader in his characters and their situation, because if he does not the reader might not go on reading, might not buy his book or borrow it from the library. In any case, his concern is very often with the emotional richness he has to uncover—for instance, in the superb mixture of positive and negative feelings in Raoul Dahl's story of a vegetarian giant, 'The BFG.' The plot is of course important and surprising; but our sympathy with the giant is what is paramount and has to be cunningly established at the outset.

Sometimes I follow this practice. In 'Why the King of the Underworld was cross' or 'The Little Gold Box,' (the only one of my stories which began life as a written narrative), the beginning is important and meant to intrigue the audience; but more often, as in the folktale, the opening words set the scene with a minimum of fuss:

> 'Once upon a time, Jonathan was having breakfast when . . .'

The teller of tales has usually no need to create an atmosphere of fantasy right at the beginning. The fact that he is there is enough. He is talking to his listeners, by definition they are interested in what he is going to say. Indeed, at the outset, they may still be a bit distracted. The cottage full of peasants is still getting beer from the can, the little girl has not quite settled herself down in bed to listen. But what gets their attention is not the teasing emotions of the opening but the expectations aroused by the presence of the story-teller.

The Jonathan stories are not, of course, folktales. They are the creation of a middle-class Anglo-Welsh poet entertaining his daughters. As a poet I learnt a lot from them: the dramatic use of poetic narrative, the delights of anachronism, the use of magic as almost another dimension of reality—a hypothetical world that, like the square root of minus one, does not really exist but you can use as if it did. As a hypothetical power it obeys its own laws as precisely as the programming of a computer. 'Third-finger magic' in 'The Wild Boy' and 'zipping' from 'The Little Gold Box' are good examples—the latter term actually borrowed from a program of computer software. Indeed, magic is to psychology what technology is to science. Advertising and publicity are in fact debased, highly successful applications of magic.

The stories, as I finally wrote them down, differ a great deal in how much they preserve the oral tale. All but one started as told stories, it is true, and I took more or less elaborate notes every time. The notes were then worked up as written narratives; but the amount of sea-change they suffered in the process varied a lot. In some, such as 'The Giant who didn't know how' and 'The Little Unicorn,' which were worked on almost immediately—and certainly within the same week—the oral story was almost unchanged. Any changes or tidying up were purely cosmetic. Other stories were left, sometimes for years, and the writing then became almost a separate creation. This is not always a question of length: 'The Wild Boy,' one of the longest and most complicated, is a very oral tale, whereas 'The Finding of Tom Glum' grew out of a rejected opening for 'The Caliph of the Stars' and (after the first two or three pages) was very largely a written affair, though I told it in the process of writing it out.

When (on a Welsh Ysgol Haf) I showed some of these tales to a fellow-student, a lady from Puffins, she seemed a bit bemused by them. She thought they had promise, but advised me to steer clear of fairies and elves and wizards: everything Tolkienesque was quite out of fashion, though apparently witches were all right. However, when I said I had no great desire to have a career as a children's writer, she lost interest. As a servant of her market, if I didn't want to play her game, she knew there were plenty that would.

Actually, the stories seem not much like Tolkien. If I had to compare them with a popular classic, it would probably be with *Alice in Wonderland*—but that's exaggerating as much in one direction as referring to *The Hobbit* in the other.

The stories take off in fact from the story of Pwyll in the

Mabinogion. Jonathan is a kind of out-of-work incomer and flute-player with a cottage in a Welsh hamlet. His dogs kill a rabbit that the King of the Underworld is hunting; and as in *Pwyll* the two change roles—but only for a week, so that the King of the Underworld can indulge his craving for making cakes. The King keeps regretting he's in the wrong job—he should have been a delicatessen baker. That's where his heart lies. Most of the fairyfolk in the stories are a bit down at heel, suburban and aging. But you can't generalise. Some of them are quite heroic. There is also a Caliph of the Stars, Obadiah Williams, D.D., who is a Southern negro with a dialect out of Mark Twain. His assistant, however, the commander of a flying saucer, is called Graham, speaks public school R.P. and is so polite no one can understand him.

There are various imps, elves, giants, dwarfs—who work in a slate quarry and suffer a lock-out—wizards, scientists and witches. And of course, mammoths and orang-utangs and tropical rain forests and a plague of butterflies and a lot about the philosophical problems of time and space. And the educational prospects if you're a giant—the dangers of work experience and Y.T. And how to make little boys out of goats and the iniquity of so doing. How to get round a lady prime minister; and how awful dragons are who want to be loved—fortunately the one in the story likes ballet so its desires can be sublimated. The gnomes are stately home-owners, opening their estates to tourists. They have statues of humans with wheel-barrows and watering cans. There are jewel thieves, helicopters, coffee mornings and how to ring up an Underworld spy, called Inkspot, in the High Mountains. And unicorns and pegasuses and three or four dogs who are central characters—Josh and Cleversticks and Tiny, and a pup called Tump. (Oddly enough, in real life I didn't particularly like dogs.) And a species of wasp that has evolved magical powers and has to be exterminated. And the King of the Underworld's lady piper whom he won't let wear a kilt because it's not proper for a woman; he is very fond of her though she will play pibrochs and laments when he is trying to get the dragon to dance.

Lastly, to say that the oral story is not driven by the desire to express emotion does not mean that it is feelingless. 'The Little

Unicorn' which was far and away the most successful of my stories with both my daughters—they asked for it dozens of times—had them leaping around with excitement. Indeed, my wife used to complain about the Jonathans that they didn't so much send the girls to sleep as wake them up!

As far as I was concerned, Marged was a nearly ideal listener. We had no television, and her capacity for following fantasy was lively and vast. She had a great sense of the absurd. With Alys, the case was slightly different. She was a story-teller herself, and our lines sometimes got crossed! But I owe both of them more artistic insight than I can express. The poems and plays I have written since owe more to telling them Jonathans than to anything else that's ever happened to me.

THE MARCH BETWEEN LYRIC AND TRAGEDY

As a boy I wrote as much drama as I did lyric. I remember without much enthusiasm a blank-verse tragedy based on Norse myth, in which the entire cast had de-fenestrated themselves by the end; also a fragmentary bedroom farce and a nativity play. So I was pretty unspecialised in those days! But then I came to college and all my drama-friends insisted I was not a bit theatrically inclined. I do not really know why they said this, but it made a deep impression on me. I am still surprised and a bit suspicious when theatre people express an interest in my work.

I have written four* pieces which ought to be considered potential or actual tragic drama. The first was 'Day Movements,' a 'radio ode' commissioned by Welsh Radio and broadcast in 1967, a version of which was published in my *Poems 1951-67*. The radio ode was a strange uncertain form dreamed up by Aneirin Talfan Davies after the war. Perhaps its most distinguished representative was R.S. Thomas's 'The Minister', but most of us at some time or other were put through our paces. Poets were commissioned to fill half an hour of broadcasting with a poetic work for three or four voices. That was the only requirement. There was virtually no feedback, and the only poet who ever got a second go was Raymond Garlick. One couldn't learn how to do it, therefore. It remained a one-off, in a strange kind of vacuum. Most people tried to make some sort of documentary drama out of their half hour. I always hated the idea of representational poetry and determined on no account to do anything so banal.

What I produced was something halfway between an abstract drama and a lieder recital without music. Like 'Under Milk

---

* This was written in 1991. I have been engaged on several plays since—'Cry at the World's End', 'Meinir and Rhys' and 'Taliesin.' 'Meinir and Rhys' is the only one to have been performed—at the Tony Conran Festival, December 1995 by Dymphra D'Arcy and Company.

Wood' its action was the doings of one day—twenty-four hours from dawn to dawn: but there the resemblance ended. It centred on the theme of resurrection, starting with lovers leaving one another, the soul shaking itself free from the half-death of modern life, Mary Magdalene going to the tomb, the dead in their graves. Then the risen Christ waiting for his guests; and following this an adaptation of Owain Cyfeiliog's 'Hirlas' poem to modern war and a tragic lament by a soldier's widow. The piece came to an end with a dream about meeting St David in the streets of Merthyr and his message that Welsh people had to wing out like wild birds over the bitter sea, as the early saints had done, to save their souls alive and regenerate their nation in the fierce humility of Bethlehem.

As well as the broadcast, student actors performed 'Day Movements' as a one-act 'play' in Bangor and Cricieth. Though it verged towards tragedy, for most of the time it stayed well this side of lyric. Different kinds of poem were set at angles to each other to produce a dramatic shape which was sometimes actually realised as tragic speech. When we later produced 'The Angry Summer' for the stage, I was pleased to find that Idris Davies had done very much the same sort of thing. Idris Davies, formally, was the most interesting of the writers on this borderland of lyric and tragic poetry; but it is a very Anglo-Welsh march, Vernon Watkins, Dylan Thomas, Glyn Jones and R.S. Thomas all furnishing interesting examples. It is a borderland quite distinct from the nearest English equivalent, the tradition of extended dramatic monologue, which is quite rare in Anglo-Welsh writing.

I called 'Day Movements' a 'choreography for voices,' and I want to talk about ritual and dance, which have meant so much in my work. Western drama twice grew out of ritual—once from the rituals of Dionysus at Athens and once from the Roman Mass in various places in mediaeval Christendom. I have of course never been involved in the Attic Dionysia; but I became a Catholic just in time to participate in the Roman Mass before it was swept aside by the Second Vatican Council. There was a sense of drama pregnant in it even then—it's a mistake to think that drama has to be verbally followed. The Mass was not just mimed, but neither was it living speech. The fragments of Latin that you heard, and the even smaller fragments you understood, were placed in a context that was totally familiar and totally exotic, at the same time. Within every Mass there was a people—a chorus—and a tragic hero. His death was inevitable, our attendance was required. His purpose was both hidden and revealed to us in the same riddling and familiar otherness of Latin. The priest was in fact an actor, in persona Christi. For most of the time he had his face turned away from us. His clothes had nothing to do with naturalism, either of contemporary life or first century Palestine. Like many of the gestures he used, they appertained originally to the habits of Roman gentlemen of the fourth century A.D. But essentially they were a mask to denote an actor who was playing, in certain metaphorical ways, the part of Christ. If you want to understand Greek tragedy, look first at the stage-figure at the altar of the Roman Mass.

It is no accident that most of the poetic tragedy of the twentieth century has been written by Catholics, either Roman or their imitations in the Anglican Church: Claudel, Lorca, Eliot, Saunders Lewis, all shared in the proto-drama of the Mass. Even Yeats, the exception that proves the rule, was a Protestant from Catholic Ireland. He idealised the peasantry and searched all his life for a ritual drama (Indian dance or Japanese Noh) almost as if he wanted a substitute for the Sunday mystery that gave shape to their lives. Eliot's most successful play is *Murder in the Cathedral* which is very close both to the form and the spirit of the Mass—so close indeed that the poet felt impelled to introduce a sermon at the proper place, between what we used to call the Mass of the Catechumens (those who were not yet baptised into the mysteries) and the sacrificial rite of the Mass proper. Eliot's attempt in his later plays to leave the Mass for the conventions of the West End Stage was certainly a failure: the further away he gets from ritual, the less dramatic reality he achieves.

The desire or temptation to 'do a Mass' is very strong in me, as I think it is in a lot of Catholic and Anglican poets. R.S. Thomas has written what he calls a Mass, limiting himself to the 'choruses'—the *kyrie, gloria, credo, sanctus, benedictus and agnus dei*—that are normally set by composers. That is a specifically lyrical response. For a dramatic poet, however, these are mere interludes:

the action itself is what matters. As Aristotle insists, tragedy is an imitation of action, not of human beings or their emotions.

Ritual is the art of community: it is by no means limited to religious rites. So I suppose this is the point where one ought to talk about the tragic chorus. However, I think I'll defer doing that until I come to 'Branwen', where it became relevant to my work for the first time as part of a tragic design.

So now, what about dance? The hatred of dance—there is no other word for it—that characterised Western society and specifically the Christian church from its birth in the post-Roman world until at least the nineteenth century is a source of astonishment and shame to me. Collingwood called dance the mother of the arts. Every other art derives from dance, or once formed the background to it. Every other art is the better for remembering dance as its inheritance. But today even educated people see no function in dance beyond physical exercise and entertainment. At least the mediaeval fear of it as devil's work was better than that!

I come from a family where dance has been important. My mother and father were excellent ballroom dancers—my uncle said of my father (whom he didn't like) that his 'brains were in his feet.' My wife is a morris dancer, my children do ballet and disco ten nights in the week. As for me, being physically spastic has made most of my imagery kinaesthetic—I have been forced to feel in terms of physical movement rather than sight or hearing. I don't dance, except in private; though when my daughters were babies I used to dance for them, to the music of Indian ragas. But my poetry I've always thought of as a dance for the tongue and the vocal chords: ultimately, since tongues and vocal chords don't occur in a vacuum, for the whole body, the whole mind. But then, all good dance is an intelligent and knowledge-giving activity; all good art is that.

I have had two 'road to Damascus' experiences in the theatre, and they both involved the union of dance, music and words. One was a review by Cranko the choreographer called simply *Cranks*. I think he put it on when he was still a student in Oxford or Cambridge, but it was taken to the West End where I saw it, I think in the middle fifties. I have never watched anything with such concentration or delight. The shapes that the different items made, both inside themselves and set off one against another so that the whole show was a kind of abstract drama, made me see the art of the theatre as if for the first time, as a dance. A dance in which words and music as well as gesture and mime had their necessary place. I had just seen a goodish performance of Sophocles' *Electra* in which, however, the chorus was the usual shambles: a lot of portentous upper-class voices making gestures towards movement. If only, I said to myself, if only . . . Surely Greek tragedy must grow out of the dance, not the other way round. Or rather, the actors are like the pianist in the slow movement of Beethoven's fourth piano concerto, they must confront the totality of the orchestra, the whole dance of the populace, with their own speech, their own dance with words. In practical terms the actors should find it easier to talk to the dancing chorus than to talk to each other. But ultimately, in Greek tragedy, the actor, the word, the poet, prevails—just as in the *Euminides* the actor who plays Pallas Athene prevails over the dancing chorus of Furies. But this is a very impressionistic way of talking: there are as many relationships between chorus and actors in Greek tragedy as there are between orchestra and soloists in concerto performance.

The other revelation I've had from the theatre was a performance of Indian drama in Liverpool. Kathakali is at once one of the simplest and one of the most sophisticated dramatic traditions in the world. There is no special stage. You can hire a performance in your back garden. It begins with two attendants holding a piece of cloth between them, and then twitching it away, letting it drop. Musicians come on, and a singer starts to sing from one of the Indian epics, the Ramayana or the Mahaberata. The actors or dancers then begin. Their make-up is so elaborate it takes three or four hours to put on. The discipline of make-up is said to be a religious preparation. Their robes also are rich and heavy. You wonder how anyone could dance at all, cluttered like this. However they dance or mime the story that is being sung, with their legs wide apart and bent like a toy cavalryman divorced from his horse. They always face the audience, because their backs are virtually naked. In India sometimes an attendant fans them to keep them cool enough to dance in the fierce heat. The actors utter no sound, except that those playing demons are sometimes allowed to grunt. When I saw them, one of their dramas was based on the Bhagavad Gita. I shall never forget how completely they realised the scene: Krishna driving the chariot for Arjuna between the two armies, telling him not to despair and revealing his own divinity. Everything was convention, every gesture, every moment; and of course I understood not a word of the song. Yet everything was so transparent, pathos, humour, exultation, devilry—even godhead. I have no doubt I was simply skimming the surface of their art but even so the clarity and liveliness was stunning. It was certainly a great theatrical experience.

Years later two New Zealand dancers, Bronwyn Judge and Anna Holmes, were living in Bangor and putting on shows together. They liked to work with poetry, as well as music. Their dance was muscular, and they used body noises, slaps, sharp spurts of breath and sometimes vocal sound. They asked me to write a poem for them to dance to; and I'm afraid they got considerably more than they bargained for. I wrote them the second of the four pieces I mentioned at the beginning, pieces that ought to be considered as potential or actual tragic drama: 'Blodeuwedd,' which was published in *Blodeuwedd and Other Poems* as a 'poem for dancing'. Basically it was a play for Kathakali. When it was performed in Bangor and Swansea two actresses recited the poem between them. We used an Irish bagpipes—the sort you play with a bellows—for occasional music, and some of the poetry was sung. At the end, when Blodeuwedd is changed into an owl, Anna danced it magnificently. She had gone to a zoo to look at eagle owls waking up. She was every inch a horned owl, an owl mask screaming for prey. I wouldn't have liked to be a mouse within range of that screech!

The trouble was, the dancers were going back to New Zealand. They hardly had time to put the show together—in fact, they left Wales with it not properly finished—let alone arrange a proper tour. The performance in Bangor went off very well, but in Swansea they had to make do with the Art Gallery, without a proper stage. People couldn't see what was happening. However, when they got to New Zealand they managed to finish the show with another actress—just one this time—and made a very successful tour with it.

In 'Day Movements' I had experimented with a kind of abstract drama, without a plot, but using a sequence of lyrics to make a dramatic shape. That is basically the medium I used for 'Blodeuwedd' too, except that all the lyrics were spoken or sung by one person and told her story. Each lyric was a separate movement, a unit having its own formal roundedness and cadence. The dramatic interaction between the characters was left to be mimed by the dancers; the poetry narrated and filled in the lyric background to what happened, a bit like the soliloquies in Macbeth.

As we were finishing 'Blodeuwedd' I told my wife Lesley that my next poem would be for morris dancers—she was at the time musician to the City of Bangor Morrismen. I'm not sure she took me seriously. But a year or so later the national Eisteddfod yr Urdd happened to be in Dyffryn Ogwen near Bangor. It was suggested that I should put on a poetry show to raise a bit of money for it. So I consulted with a musician friend, and before we knew what we were doing I was writing a five act tragedy with song and dance routines to be organised by my friend. I am afraid that as a fund-raiser for the Urdd *Branwen* was a disastrous failure. I hadn't written more than two acts by the deadline. Things went wrong almost from the start. I couldn't get the musician to write any music; finally he dropped out altogether. I was left with a dramatic fragment on my hands, whose very conception relied on dance and music, without a composer and without a choreographer. So I buckled down to it. Although I don't have any musical training I did know a lot about folksong and enough about morris to find out more. The City of Bangor Morrismen included some very knowledgeable people at that time: one man in particular, an ex-monk who had been teaching in Nigeria, a man full of *duende*, a dancer in his bones. He understood what I wanted almost before I told him and actually organised a mock-up of Yorkshire long-sword in Llanberis because he knew I wanted to see what it was like. The dancers in general had no trouble apprehending why I wanted to use morris or in appreciating its emotional range.

Morris is not just one kind of dance. It is comparable to a whole family of languages. In Britain there are six main classes and within each class local traditions are like dialects, each with its own style and way of doing things. Cotswold morris, which was the one that caught the fancy of Cecil Sharp and is therefore the best known, is essentially a rural dance; but the morris of the North-West (Lancashire and Cheshire) is associated with the Wakes Weeks of industrial towns. Rapper or Short-sword is danced by Northumberland miners, Long-sword by Yorkshire iron-workers. The two other classes are Border and Molly. Welsh morris was a dialect of Border, usually called the Cadi Ha from the name of its principal attendant, the man-woman, Cadi Ha(f) or Summer Kathy. Morris is therefore not specifically an English dance nor a specifically rural one. Dances like it are found on the Continent, particularly in the industrialised Basque Country of Northern Spain.

The morris 'languages' are very varied, both in physical terms and in their emotional effect. The North-West expresses the group's power and confidence as it marches out into the world. Cotswold imitates the vaunting and playful struggles within the group. Rapper gives us the seamless co-operation of men bound together by skill and danger—the group there is more introverted and the music is fast. But what they have in common is that all of them are danced by a defined and exclusive team, six or eight men together. The morris is not a community affair like a ring dance or a reel. Nobody but a proper morrisman can join in. In musical terms it is a choir not a congregation. Neither of course is it a dance to express personal inwardness, like ballet. There are solo dances ('jigs') in Cotswold morris, but they are not usually even Cock o' the Wall affairs like the Norwegian Halling. They are merely show pieces for a good dancer, or interludes to give the team time to rest. Morris is an expression of a male group (and as such very male-chauvinist) but it is offered for the entertainment of others. Its ethos is one of benevolent equality: feelings of aggression and contempt are contained in ritualised play. This ethos is not something imposed from outside, but confident and obvious in any morris performance.

The morris is already quasi-dramatic. The often weird clothes that the dancers wear, the frequent habit of blacking their faces, and the stylised buffoonery they often affect, all add to this theatrical presence. Teams are often accompanied by 'attendants'—a fool, a man dressed as a woman, a hobby-horse. Sometimes they perform an actual mummer's play about St George or Robin Hood. Maid Marion was originally a morris man-woman, a Cadi Ha, imported into Sherwood from the morrismen's mumming. And of course the dance was associated with the Elizabethan theatre. It is likely that the first night of King Lear ended with a morris-dance.

When I wrote *Branwen* I wanted drama to grow out of the dance, very much as Greek tragedy did; and the choice of morris as a matrix offered several advantages. Like all popular drama—pantomime, Punch and Judy, music hall—morris and mumming play are profoundly anachronistic. Lord Nelson or Henry VIII rub shoulders with Mrs Thatcher or Jack the Ripper. I wanted to use eleventh-century Welsh stories in a play about Revolution. Brân, without ceasing to be a legendary giant, was to be a revolutionary leader, with the dancers representing the revolutionary populace. The morris actually simplifies this process by imposing a stylised theatricality right from the start. It introduces and embodies the no-place and no-time where the play is enacted—the 'two neighbouring Third World countries: Ancient Britain and the Kingdom of Ireland.'

Second, the morris imposed its own ethos—sexist but benevolent, hopeful and group-oriented—as the norm against which both Branwen, a woman betrayed by unthinking masculine opportunism, and Efnisien, the isolated male villain, find themselves as tragic protagonists. The morris norm is symbolised by a totem figure, the Crow, carried round by the morrismen like a hobby horse. The Crow represents Brân the leader, a giant who never actually appears on stage (*brân* means crow in Welsh); but in a very real sense the play is as much Brân's tragedy as it is Branwen's or Efnisien's.

Third, the various 'languages' of morris could be used to

express a range of feelings—determination to resist aggression, self-confidence, celebration, drunkenness, dismay or the finality of broken hope—as they arose in the play. These feelings were not forced on the dancers, they came from a combination of the physical movements of the dance and the situation on stage.

Fourth, the reality of the dance made it possible for other effects—songs, choral speaking, chanting—to arise without awkwardness. In the morris environment these things seem to occur naturally. Though I rarely had the dancers sing together yet their presence as a chorus could be felt. From the moment they processed onto the stage singing the 'Cadi Ha' song, the revolutionary populace was real. It had a shape and a direction. It had a voice.

Fifth, the traditional attendants on the morris gave me a useful purchase on the action. I have mentioned the Crow, a substitute for the hobbyhorse. There was also the Cadi Ha himself, the man in drag. These two, the wordless leader and the eloquent led, are not characters in the normal sense. They are ciphers who act out whatever role the action demands—buffoonery, political rhetoric or 'normal' human responses. The Crow is only Brân at second hand, so to speak. He can only speak through the other members of the cast. Neither Crow nor Cadi should be imaginable outside the cock-and-bull world of the morris performance. They are part of the charade-like fantasy associated with the dance—half tomfoolery, half degenerate archetypes of the gods.

If you look at Punch and Judy or Pantomime, what you see are not actors in the normal sense of the word, but stage-figures imitating action. They have no inwardness as human beings. It is the same with the mumming plays. Characters are introduced like this—

> Here comes I the bold Turkish knight.
> I came from the Turkish land to fight.
> First I fought in England,
> And then I fought in Spain,
> And now I am come back to England,
> To fight St George again.
> If I could meet St George here

> I would put my spear in through his ear,
> I would beat him and bale him
> And cut him in slices
> And take a small pot and make a pair of garters.

Clearly to apply Method acting to such a personage is a category mistake. If I was to let my drama grow out of the morris, what I had to do was to find a tragic and poetic equivalent of the Turkish knight. It is stage-figures, not Method actors, who must emerge from the dance.

I began all right. There is a riddling kind of prologue before the dancers enter, where Branwen and Manawydan seem to be in a kind of dream about their childhood and only begin to engage in real dialogue towards the end. Then the clatter of the morris announces Revolution. As the dust clears, the two twins, Efnisien and Nisien, snipe at each other from opposite sides of the stage:

> 'What a palaver of honours for Brân tonight!'

> 'His sword has won it. His right deserves it.'

> 'Oversize gipsy! King over tinkers!'

> 'King over Britain—the people claim him!'

In comes I, the Turkish knight . . . Of course, you can't continue like this for very long without *rigor mortis* setting in. You have to soften the outlines, invest your figures with humanity, tenderness, the ability to make mistakes. But up to the fourth act they remain stage figures imitating action. They could at a pinch have worn masks.

But then in Act IV the scene changes to the court of the Irish king who has married Branwen and is now battering her. (That is more or less in the *Mabinogion*.) Nisien who has been banished by Brân turns up and finds Branwen being punched by her husband. It was difficult to remember that these were just stage figures and not people. The morris had been left behind in Britain, so my novel-haunted imagination was naked. I think I overstepped the mark. Branwen and Nisien suddenly seem persons, they look into themselves, they have insides, inwardness.

Of course, in one way, the drama takes off at this point. I became aware of what it is to be a dramatist, not just a tragic poet. Nor do I oppose inwardness as such—'Blodeuwedd' is a very inward-looking, not to say introvert, poem. But the contemporary dance of Bronwyn and Anna was a very different kettle of fish from morris. I am not sure: partly because, when the students in Bangor workshopped 'Branwen' almost up to performance level, morris and all, I had not finished Act V in time for them to act it. I have never seen Act V in any of its versions done with morris. And therefore I do not know if the play is recoverable as a dance drama.

What happened next can be simply told. Gilly Adams of the Made in Wales Stage Company had worked with Graham Laker on the students' workshop production, and after considerable time and trouble on both our parts we agreed that she should produce the play professionally, without morris, but using music. She urged me to do so because the chances of a production with dancers were extremely slim, and I don't think she ever thought the morris was necessary to the success of the play.

Of course she was right: the play worked as a verse play about a family. The revolution was not off-stage, though it never quite felt at the dramatic centre. The Cadi and Crow dichotomy was dissolved but in the theatre the Cadi's unexplained presence was not distracting.

One of the benefits of her production was that I was encouraged to attend rehearsals. If things were wrong with the text I could work at revising it with the actors or the musicians. I added at least two scenes, and wrote new songs. Act V in particular I had left very sketchy and it was a great help to work on it in this way. But inevitably these revisions and additions took me further and further away from the dance-drama I had originally written.

ANGELOGICAL

ANGELOLOGICAL

I.m. Peter Hoy, Fellow of Merton

Bangor, dear city of angels!—
The sad anguish it has gone
Like thought, like a secret thought
In the ebbtide of morning.

We were young angels then. Books
Would be written, were present,
Were already in the world—
Angelological journals,
Cherubic notebooks, Poems
Englished from the Seraphim:
Principalities and Powers
Attended on our book launch.

An angel is where it thinks.
It has no need of recall.
Gabriel wants no memory
To kneel in annunciation.
The Last Trump is at his lips.
Lucifer, the morning Star,
Cannot choose but be falling,
Falling, falling, for the fall
Contaminates his thinking—
Where he is—to the extent
Of time, duration of place.

An angel is where it thinks.
Infinity of cherubs
Laugh at the same joke, lament
Over one sparrow's mishap.
Seraphim with sleepless eye
Veil their God-ravished faces
With the long wings' flight-feathers.
They have watched out the big bang.
They see beyond the light years
To the exploding Nothing.
Their art clears the primal soup,
The opaqueness of creation.

Peter, it was only last week
I finished one intention:
The Angelogical Notebook
Lay flush in the printing tray.
DOS and format and WordStar
Had revealed and done their worst.
This was your book. To no one
Else, mon confrère, dear angel,
Would it be dedicated
In the public domain of print.

And then the phone. You were dead.
The crying perturbation
Of what to do with a life
Ransacked from so much learning
Faltered in the receiver.
No angel can claim such grief.
Already you were fading
Out of reach of your thought.
Problematic where you were—
Moulted, tail and flight-feathers.
Did you kneel? Were there trumpets
Tongued flashingly in the wind?
Now you can never be sent
Angelological journals,
Fading, and merely human
Not where your thought is—dead, dead,
In the wisp of a white body
That the savage heart has torn.